Remedies for the Heart

ANITRA FREENEY

ISBN 978-1-0980-9898-8 (paperback)
ISBN 978-1-0980-9899-5 (digital)

Copyright © 2021 by Anitra Freeney

All rights reserved. No part of this publication may be reproduced, distributed, or transmitted in any form or by any means, including photocopying, recording, or other electronic or mechanical methods without the prior written permission of the publisher. For permission requests, solicit the publisher via the address below.

Christian Faith Publishing, Inc.
832 Park Avenue
Meadville, PA 16335
www.christianfaithpublishing.com

Printed in the United States of America

Contents

Foreword 5
Preface 7

Chapter 1: Value 9
Chapter 2: Keep Thine Heart 22
Chapter 3: It's All about Him 32
Chapter 4: In Him 49
Chapter 5: A Renewed Mindset 68
Chapter 6: Moving On 76

A Word from the Author 81
Prayer of Salvation 83

Foreword

Boy am I excited about this new book *Remedies for the Heart*. Matthew 4:19 says, "Follow me and I will make you fishers of men." *Remedies for the Heart* is nothing more than a well-constructed tackle box filled with all the bait Anitra needs to be a successful fisherman of men for the Lord. Each chapter holds truths and nuggets that will catch those who are in dire need of being caught. While she elaborates on life situations and circumstances, they aren't the focus of this book. The primary focus of this book is to let you know despite the things you've been through, there are remedies for the heart that will help activate the God within you and inform you of His ability to keep you. Undoubtedly, you will make it if you surrender to God and let Him do what only He can do: mend your heart. May God bless you and keep you is our prayer.

—Rev. Kennon L. Tenison
Senior Pastor, Pleasant Hill Missionary Baptist Church

Preface

Carefully constructed through self-reflection, this book details promises from God to overcome hurts that everyday common people experience. Through my personal short stories, I elaborate on applying biblical principles to realize and walk in the God-granted victory given to every believer.

These anecdotes tell of how I am currently overcoming negative emotions exacerbated by not fully understanding the promises and victory granted to me as by-products of the death, burial, and resurrection of Jesus Christ, my personal Lord and Savior.

Feelings of despair, abandonment, fear, inferiority, shame, and loneliness can all be defeated by the use of the unfailing, noncontradictory Word of God. When we bring these negative thoughts into captivity and make them obey Christ, awesome and powerful movement takes place (2 Corinthians 10:5).

Chapter 1

Value

> But the very hairs of your head are all numbered. Do not fear; therefore, you are of more *value* than many sparrows.
> —Luke 12:7 (NKJV)

Labels, Security Tags, Name Brands—Oh My!

I recently had the opportunity to work for a clothing store. While it was nothing like my career choice in education, I couldn't negate the fact that it was a resource to meet a need. I needed a car and I needed additional money to purchase a car. Having saved enough money and finding myself in a wee bit of a heated disagreement with my boss, I resigned. Never did I think that a part-time job could be used to see a simplistic spiritual truth.

During the time I worked, I quickly discovered one of the most time-consuming tasks was removing the security tags. Not every security tag was the same, and not every item had a security tag on it. I quickly learned the criteria for the varying types of security tags. Most items purchased at a low price weren't accompanied by security tags; however, moderately priced items would most definitely have one of the simpler security tags attached to it. However, as we all know, discounted stores often have designer labels at a lower price. The value of these items was so highly esteemed they could often be found in the designer section on a different rack. Now these items, whether they were clothes, shoes, or handbags, all came with one to two security tags on them. It wasn't uncommon to have to remove the normal run of the mill security tag and then must remove an additional tag known as a screamer. If placed within a certain number of feet of the security device at the door, a shrill scream would emanate from the item causing all shoppers and employees alike to stop and stare (I was guilty of unintentionally leaving one on a couple of times). Obviously the store manager, etc. knew the worth of the item and as such, went to various measures to ensure just not anyone could walk out of the store without paying for it. In other words, they wanted to make sure the item's worth was appreciated. If we can go to these steps to ensure materialistic items, which can very easily become too small, too large, or worn, are appreciated and aren't tampered with, how much more should we appreciate ourselves?

It's no secret that I formerly struggled with a poor self-image and often succumbed to the effects of low self-esteem, but it was only because I didn't know my worth. I didn't know I was a designer label and came with the ultimate security tag. I didn't know I shouldn't have been placing myself on the regular clearance racks instead of resting elegantly in the designer section. I just didn't know. Oh, but I now know. Not only am I designer, but I am also tailor-made, one of a kind, an original. No, I'm not being conceited; no, I'm not being cocky. I can prove it to you.

Psalm 139:13–16 (MSG) states,

> Oh yes, you shaped me first inside, then out; you formed me in my mother's womb. I thank you, High God—you're breathtaking! Body and soul, I am marvelously made! I worship in adoration—what a creation! You know me inside and out, you know every bone in my body; You know exactly how I was made, bit by bit, how I was sculpted from nothing into something. Like an open book, you watched me grow from conception to birth; all the stages of my life were spread

out before you, the days of my life all prepared before I'd even lived one day.

You see, God so intricately wove me together to be the me that I am. He took His time and *designed* me as He saw fit. There very well may be another Anitra Lachelle on the face of this earth, but I guarantee you, she and I are two different people. She may even look like me, but again, we each are tailor-made. We each are a designer product. God took His time and put each of us together specifically the way He envisioned it. Why then do we allow anyone and everyone to handle us? Why don't we go and sit as the special creations we are? Why don't we place value on ourselves? Why don't we allow God to be our security tags and keep us? Many designer labels don't advertise too much. They rest in knowing that upon seeing the creation or item, the quality of the product will speak for itself. They don't feel the need to talk about what their label stands for or how great the clothing item will feel on you, they simply trust that the time and effort put into creating it will show forth its beauty.

Just remember, we weren't placed on an assembly line and mass-produced; each one of us was painstakingly woven together one at a time way before we were even thought of. Don't continue to live a life of "I'm not good enough. I'm not pretty enough. I'm not fine enough. I'm not model-sized." Yes, we can all do what is necessary to be healthy, but ultimately, we are gorgeous simply because our Designer created us in that way.

Imperfectly Invaluable

The green digits on the clock glowed and informed me that it was merely three fifty-nine in the morning. My sleep was brought to an abrupt end with the words, "You have value." No, there wasn't anyone in my bed with me. No, I don't experience delusions, hallucinations, or psychotic episodes involving voices. I know whose voice it was because I know to whom I belong. I've been wrestling for quite some time with my issue. Period, point-blank, I don't like it. I don't like what it means for my life. I actually hate it. I hate what it does to my mind, to my relationships, and to my overall disposition. I *hate it*. I feel that it detracts from who I am and hinders people from being able to treat me normally. It makes me feel worthless.

During a conversation yesterday, I expounded on these feelings and how I wish I didn't have certain personality quirks. My mind is quite a unique entity and unfortunately, when left to its own devices, does some pretty intense projections and what-if scenarios. I tire of this; honestly, I do. As I talked—more like belabored my frustration with overanalyzing and overthinking things—my conversation partner simply leaned forward and, in what seemed like a whisper, said, "What if the things you don't like about yourself are actually the things that make you gifted and unique?" She went on to explain that the very things I dislike the most are the very things that come together and allow a person named Anitra to be. In essence, the things I would like to change about myself are the very things at the core of who I am. To say I dislike those things is to say I dislike me. Not cool, huh?

So I returned to my home, my haven, my humble abode where all my thinking and creative juices freely flow, and I sat in it for a moment. I simply sat and thought, *All the things that I find difficult to live with make up my giftedness. Wait a minute, I'm gifted? I'm not messed up beyond repair? My issue isn't a hindrance? I'm not handicapped and unable to coexist with those who don't have a label? My giftedness can overpower my label?* As my day went on, I had other things and obligations to attend to, so I allowed the thought to simply linger, as most thoughts do, in my head. I'd actually forgotten about it and was completely in awe of one of my accomplishments for the day. Sleep didn't come easy, as I was completely amped about my day. Typically, when I take my sleep aid, I *sleep* to the point of having to set multiple alarms so that I don't oversleep. I'm not easily awakened; I don't really toss or turn, or so I'm told. No, none of that; I get my sleep in. However, at 3:59 a.m., I heard that still, serene voice simply say, *You have value.* As I sat up in my bed, I thought about that, ran to the restroom, and jumped back in my bed so that I could go back to sleep, or so I thought. No, my mind did its usual and began to bounce all around the place, but it was focused on one thing. Why do I have value? Who says I have value? What do I say to myself when I feel like I am without value? As I was literally bothered, I began to pray. *Lord, help me understand my value and live up to it. Let me not allow people to treat me as less than, but more importantly, don't allow me to treat me as less than.* By now, it is somewhere around 4:30 a.m., and I am still awake! As my conversation with God continued, He began to give me just what I needed.

Here is what I heard and understood this concept of value to mean for me.

The value of a thing or being isn't found internally. No, the value is found in how much someone on the outside is willing to pay, sacrifice, give, or give up for the thing or being. Do you see where I'm going? At auctions, art galleries, even car lots, the most precious things require quite a bit of money to obtain them. At an auction, the people bidding on the item have in their minds an idea of how much the thing is worth to them individually. Each person has an idea, a price, a quote, and the one who sees it and qualifies it as being worth whatever pays the price and obtains the item. Along these lines, I'm reminded of the game show *Let's Make a Deal*. On this show, people make a deal based on a description of a possible package. Monty Hall, the host, if memory serves me correctly, would say that the prize was *valued* in the amount of $__. The contestant would then have to decide if what they had in their hand was worth trading for the possibility of something greater. They had to deem the value of the package worthy of a sacrifice.

Many, many years ago, Christ deemed me worthy of so much value that His life was worth sacrificing for mine. He, in his ability to see beyond the present, looked at me, the package, covered in filth and sin and said, "That's my NeeNee (a childhood nickname). Yes, she is worth my life. That girl right there is an asset to the kingdom, and I will literally give my all that she may live and live more abundantly." While that sounds amazingly selfish, it gives me courage, strength, and surrounds me with love—to know someone invaluable, sinless, perfect, and divine calls me worthy and valuable. There isn't too much a person can say to make me think otherwise, and there shouldn't be a person who can say something to you that would make you feel otherwise.

I don't have value because I graduated as salutatorian and received associate's, bachelor's, and master's degrees. I don't have value because someone is my friend, because I'm a Freeney, or because of any of those things. I, like you, have value because Christ literally laid down His life for me. He counted and still counts me worthy even in those moments when I hate myself. He counts me worthy and invaluable when people walk away. He counts me worthy when people say she can't, won't, and shouldn't be able to do that. He looks at me and knows—not just sees, not just thinks, but knows—that little chocolate girl right there is a force to be reckoned with. He counted me worthy and invaluable way before my parents even knew they were having their fourth child.

He counts me worthy, period, point-blank.

Identity Crisis

"Tell me about yourself." These four words used to cause me to cringe upon hearing them. I never could figure out exactly how to talk about myself because I didn't know who I was. You see, for so long, I have struggled with and been smack-dab in the middle of an identity crisis.

An identity crisis is a period when a person becomes uncertain or confused about who they are and the role they play in their own life. One who is dealing with a crisis of identity is one who could also be labeled as being unsettled and insecure. This lack of knowledge of who they are prevents them from being assured and confident about *anything*, especially themselves! Think about a person with amnesia. They are left to the devices of others to determine who they are and are then forced to live per what others say about them, whether it is true or not. Not knowing who you are leaves you dependent on external sources to affirm you and give life. Not a good look and most certainly not a good way to live.

So experiencing an identity crisis, I would always begin to stutter and speak incomprehensible and unintelligible words when someone inquired about my identity and who I was. I simply had no idea of how to answer that question because I didn't know who I was! Quite often, I'd start my response with what I knew to be true about myself. "Well, my name is Anitra, and I'm the youngest of four children. I'm a teacher and have been teaching for sixteen years now." I'd let that hang in the air as I presumptuously awaited follow-up questions. God forbid they didn't ask a question; I'd have no idea where to take the conversation. Thanks be to God, people would always want to know about my teaching career. That was my saving grace.

You see, my identity was wrapped up in my career, but that is not the essence of who I am. That's just something I do. Being the youngest of four children describes my birth order, but it doesn't tell you anything about who I am. As you can see, I had no idea of who I was or anything about myself for that matter. It took some (many) years, but I finally realized I needed to take some time to figure out who in the world I was.

My journey started about four or five months ago when I realized I didn't like the way my life was going as it was losing momentum and traction. I was becoming bored with just about everything I was doing, except writing, but we'll get to that in a moment.

It's common knowledge that people talk about you, positively and negatively, in your face and behind your back. Trust me, words are being shared. Though people are speaking, you determine whether their opinions become truths or just remain idle thoughts that lack power. You see, because I didn't know who I was, I allowed what others said about me to define me. The words others spoke of me from childhood would later become the opinions I would conform to.

For the longest period of my life, I can remember feeling invisible and unaccounted for. I feel I didn't get enough of my parents' attention as a child. They only took notice of me when I received an academic accomplishment that would go on to cause me to have a spirit of perfectionism, which is not of God. Perfectionistic ways are in direct opposition to salvation. If we were perfect, that would mean we were free from sin and, as a result, in no need of being saved.

Anyway, back to this identity thing. Your identity is how you describe the essence of who you are, your personality, and your being.

It is the positive rock-solid assurance of who you are and what you stand for. It is in your identity that you have formed opinions about yourself. My pastor has a saying, "Whether you think you can or can't, either way, you're right. Whether you think you are or aren't, either way, you're right." I love to hear him talk about that. He is such an awesome proclaimer of the Word.

You see, we respond to what we think and what we hold in our hearts. "Keep thy heart with all diligence; for out of it are the issues of life" (Proverbs 4:23). The heart is the organ solely responsible for the circulation of blood in your body. It is this organ that allows other organs to function and sustain life. What's in your heart? When you're all alone, what do you say to yourself about yourself? What is your self-talk like? How do you identify yourself?

So, as I have admitted, I was in dire need of help with my identity. I used to dream of hiring someone to help me transform into a beautiful young woman. See, right there, I didn't think I was beautiful as I was. I would look in the mirror and find blemishes instead of beauty, problems instead of promise. I was in an identity crisis. I didn't know whose I was and consequently didn't know who I was. I'd allowed those unfounded opinions of others to force me into a tiny box I didn't belong in.

You see, God created each of us for a purpose, and He will see it to completion until the day of Christ. We aren't entities meant to be stagnant. No, we are to be ever-evolving individuals always in pursuit of greatness. Within each of us lies so much potential, but it goes untapped until we realize there are promises for our potential.

How do you respond when someone asks you to tell them about yourself? Are you assured of who you are? Do you know your essence and purpose?

I'll tell you what I've learned about myself while on this journey. I've realized that I'm an awesome young lady. I'm beautiful inside and out, not only when I wear makeup, not only when my hair is fixed all cute but all the time. I'm beautiful when I wake up first thing in the morning. I'm beautiful when I'm dog-tired after working with other people's kids all day. I'm pretty fab even when I have my spells of depression. I'm amazing while amid an anxiety attack. How and why would I say those things about myself? I can say those things because of the Word of God. You see, He, God, affirmed me when He said I was fearfully and wonderfully made. Marvelous are His works. I am His work, and I'm simply marvelous. God has blessed me and gifted me to be able to use words in a way that not only blesses me but blesses others and hopefully brings them into a closer relationship with Him.

So if someone were to ask me to tell them about myself, what would my current response be? I'll be honest, I don't have it all figured out, but one thing I know, "My name is Anitra, and I'm falling more in love with myself each day. I love to write and aspire to be a published author one day. I'm currently on a journey to find my true identity and love the person I am and have been created to be."

What would your response be? Remember, your identity is tied directly to what you hold in your heart. Release fear, release hurt, release anger, release any and everything that would cause you to put yourself down. God is an affirming and loving God. Allow His love to permeate your heart. Don't fight His love! One of my friends loves to encourage people by telling them, "There isn't anything you can do to make God love you any more or less." If I could tag in where she leaves off, I would simply add, "His love is at maximum capacity, and there isn't anything you can do about it."

Mistaken Identity

There was once a fable told about an eagle who sadly thought he was a chicken. If you've never read it, google it. The symbolism is astounding!

You see, in the fable, there is a poor little eagle who, through no fault of his own, grew up thinking, behaving, and living as though he were a chicken. Clueless to what was really within him, he'd never flown, never soared, never even left the ground. He was bound to limits that were *never* intended to be a part of his life story.

You see, the eagle ended up in the chicken coop as a result of being mishandled. There was an ignorant farmer who failed to appreciate the beauty in what had to have been noticeable differences between the eagle and the rest of his chickens. This farmer when approached by an individual called the naturalist who had correct insight still failed to see the eagle as nothing more than an average run-of-the-mill chicken. Eventually, the eagle would have to be taken away (that's key) from the familiar territory of the coop to realize he was more than just a chicken. The eagle had to be both *removed* and *renewed* by the naturalist who had a trained eye and intuition to truly accept his calling and purpose in life. This naturalist knew the eagle wasn't a chicken. He could simply look at it and tell. It took him three tries to get the eagle to see that he was not what he'd been convinced he was. As I mentioned above, he literally took the eagle away from the chicken coop, the other chickens, and the farmer just so that he could see he was so much more than what'd he'd been living as. This eagle was suffering from a case of mistaken identity.

By now I'm sure you can see where I'm going with this, but indulge me; allow me to explain. I'm far too excited to stop now.

So let's go back to the eagle and explore some biblical truths. There are two key scriptures:

> But you are a chosen race, a royal priesthood, a holy nation, a people for his possession, that you may proclaim the excellencies of him who called you out of darkness into his marvelous light. (1 Peter 2:9)

> And be not conformed to this world, but be transformed by the renewing of your mind, that you may prove what is that good and acceptable and perfect will of God. (Romans 12:2)

In 1 Peter 2:9, the naturalist came along with one purpose in mind: to call out the eagle. The naturalist had heard of an eagle living the life of a chicken and went to check it out for himself. Upon making it to the farm, the naturalist first conversed with the farmer then the eagle. Twice, the eagle refused to hear the naturalist and returned to the chicken coop where he was comfortable with his other chicken friends. The naturalist looked at the eagle and spoke to his spirit, but the eagle didn't receive what the naturalist had to say. It wasn't until the naturalist took the eagle away from his comfort zone that the eagle did receive what the naturalist had to say. The eagle had to be called out and separated to realize he was capable of so much more than what he'd been living as. Now that's the first part of that scripture, but can't you imagine just how much the eagle went on to tell others of this wonderful man who called him out of the chicken life and pushed him into his wonderful life as an eagle. The naturalist called the eagle out of darkness into wonderful light. I'd dare say the eagle soared around, telling everyone of his life transformation and mind renewal. Like the eagle, at some point in our lives, God came along and called us out. He didn't have to hear about us. He knows us. He chose us, and He wants us to have an abundant life. His Word tells us just that. John 10:10 (NKJV) says, "The thief does not come except to steal, and to kill, and to destroy. I have come that they may have life and that they may have it more abundantly." I think it's fair to say that we have accepted Christ, but we haven't truly accepted our new lives. Maybe He is ever-so-gently tugging at your spirit and trying to convince you that you're not a chicken; you're an eagle. Listen to Him! He's right! Allow Him to call you out of darkness into wonderful light. Spread your wings and fly.

In Romans 12:2, for the eagle to accept the call to be an eagle, he had to take on a new mindset. His mind had to be renewed. As long as he could look back at the chicken coop and see his chicken friends clucking and scratching at the dirt, he longed to be with them, but the moment the naturalist took him away on top of the farmhouse, the eagle finally heard the naturalist's words and renewed his mind. His old way of thinking went out the window, and he accepted the words the naturalist had previously spoken to him. Sometimes we must be separated to become our best selves. Literally, the eagle had to be elevated to see himself the way the naturalist saw him. He had to be taken out of what was common and familiar to him to develop his new mindset. At the beginning of the story, the naturalist said that when he looked at the eagle, he knew the eagle was born an eagle, had the heart of an eagle, and nothing could change that. My goodness! When God looks at us, He says no, they were born victorious and have the heart of a victor, and nothing can change that! Glory! My pastor often teaches us about relationships and how being in the wrong relationship causes you unnecessary pain, strife, and can ultimately stunt your growth. Shaking my head yes, it is clear to see that this eagle was undoubtedly stunted in its growth. Wings were forced to remain bent, the sharpness of his talons going unused and untapped, the power in its beak waning, the strength of his wings downplayed. The potential of this eagle had never even been assessed let alone reached.

How much are we like this eagle? We have remained in comfortable positions, relationships, and even thought patterns so long that we've begun living life as though we are someone else. We've adopted other people's personas, ideals, morals, theories, and even lifestyles as our own. God is simply saying, "I'm calling you out for the life I intended you to live. Come out of what is comfortable and soar. You are who I say you are."

Perhaps you, like me, haven't always viewed yourself in the highest light. You've allowed the familiarity of your surroundings and those around you to limit you. You're so much more than you think, but you've been scratching the ground and clucking around so long it's just easier. *No!* Easy is sleazy, and it's not God's way. Was it "easy" for Christ to take on our sins and die? I think not!

I'll be the first to raise my hand and say the life I'm living is not quite at the level God would have me be, and it's not anyone's fault but my own, but this isn't about assigning blame, it's about extending our wings and soaring. It's about taking on our new identities and behaving as the eagles we are.

Allow God to call you out; allow Him to separate you, and allow your mind to be renewed daily. Shed the old behaviors. This very well may mean you end up in unfamiliar territory with newness all around you. That's okay; the one who called you out is both ever-present and all-knowing. He equips those He calls for the very work He called them for! Don't continue in a mistaken identity. Take on your new identity and live the life you were predestined for!

Prayer

Dear God, please forgive me for the times when I lived my life without regard to who you created me to be. Forgive me for not esteeming myself in you. Thank you for the awesome creation you created me to be. During the times when I feel inferior, help me to cling to Psalm 139:14. Thank you for lifting my spirit and helping me to understand exactly who I am in you.

Amen.

Reflections

After reading Chapter 1,

_____
_____
_____
_____
_____
_____
_____
_____
_____
_____
_____
_____
_____
_____

Chapter 2

Keep Thine Heart

> Keep your heart with all diligence, for out
> of it spring the issues of life.
> —Proverbs 4:23 (NKJV)

Matters of the Heart

Lately, I've had a few things on my mind and my heart. I've been just a tad bit heavy and have been fighting to remain positive. Last night, as I was in bed preparing to fall asleep, a profound thought crossed my mind with such gravity and force I had to make a note in my phone so that I wouldn't forget it.

You see, a while ago, I ran across a meme that simply said, "When God puts something on your heart, trust it means it is on His heart too." That stuck with me, and I'm glad it did, for it and my mind-blowing thought from last night are the basis of this text.

As usual, I dare not blog without a scriptural reference. Today's reference is 1 Peter 5:7 which to summarize simply says cast all your cares on Him for He cares for you. At some point, I read a version that said casting the whole of your care on Him. I love that version.

You see, I care *a lot* about people, about people's perception of me, about life's circumstances, and sadly, about things that are out of my control. With all this on my mind and in my heart, can I honestly say I have room to accept God's love? Good question, right? You see, quite often, we are found saying things like, "God knows my heart." Yes, He does, but do you know His? Do you know His character? Do you know the insurmountable amount of love His heart holds for you? Do you realize you, despite what you've been told and how you've been treated, aren't an afterthought?

How do I know there is that amount of love in God's heart? The Bible tells me, "For God so loved the world that He gave His only begotten Son, that whosoever believeth in Him shall have eternal life." Guess what! That's a promise straight from God that you can stand on.

Anyway, on to my life-changing thought from last night. Here is what popped in my head as I rested my head on my pillows and began to recount the day and its events. Life is *not* about God knowing my heart. Rather, it is about me knowing His heart and the fact that He has my best interests at the center of His heart. This is in direct parallel to 1 Peter 5:7. When I cast the whole of my care on Him, I can rest assured that He will do the rest. It is His heart that allows Him to care for me. In caring for me, He won't let anything befall me that He hasn't already brought me through.

So what about you? Shall you begin to cast your care onto God? Will you trust His heart? Remember, it's not about what is in our hearts. It's about His heart and the fact that it is filled with love toward us. Challenge yourself to fall in love with God's heart and the essence of who He is! It'll change your entire life!

Like Layers of an Onion

I recently took to Facebook and posted my heartfelt thoughts regarding my understanding of my best self. Here is what I posted:

What is the best version of you? When you stop and think about all the possibilities, daydreams, visions, and ideas you've had, what is stopping you? Who are you really? What happened that you changed? I went on to comment about how I've lost sight of who I am as a result of allowing people's opinions of me to weigh heavily on both my mind and in my heart.

Having lost sight of my true self, you know the real me, I now am on a path of rediscovering myself, but I secretly wonder if the *old* me even was the *true* me. Like have I ever really been authentic, or have I always lived life as a copy of someone else? Did I clone myself after someone? I like to hear people say things about how "real" they are. How original they are in their thought patterns and lifestyle. I'd dare pick an argument and say they're lying—"Liar, liar pants on fire!" You see, here is what I know. We are raised in an environment that helps formulate our ideals, principles, morals, and worldview. How we are raised has a lot to do with the kind of people we become. No, I'm not saying it defines us because we know we have both the proclivity and capability to change and not become a product of our environment, but it *does* shape us to a certain extent.

I was raised in a two-parent household where my father was practically a silent stakeholder. He worked, *worked*, and worked but did extraordinarily little with us (his four daughters) emotionally, spiritually, or even physically. I *cannot* remember ever hugging my dad until he was unresponsive on his deathbed. Because of this, my first marriage was *just* like my parents' marriage. I was the boss, and my ex-husband did whatever he was told and asked of him. Now in direct opposition to that, my second marriage was crazy. Because I wanted a take-charge man who knew how to be the boss, I found myself entangled with a giant who would later go on to become an ogre ruling his kingdom and demanding respect from his subjects. Do you see how my environment shaped my decision-making process? Crazy, right?

Fast-forward some years (I honestly can't remember how many) later and here I am trying to figure out just who Anitra Lachelle Freeney is. You know the beautiful woman who is buried beneath layers and layers of hurt, pain, confusion, upsets, victories, failures, and defeat. Through trials, mistakes, lessons learned, and tribulations triumphed, I've come to know *some* things about myself, but there are layers to me that have yet to be peeled back, hence the title of this text, "Like Layers of an Onion."

You see, I'm a bit of a thinker (I know this one thing about myself); I fall asleep thinking, planning, and/or strategizing. They say it's a part of being bipolar (the mind doesn't ever stop clicking and firing), but I think I'm just uniquely created this way for a purpose. I've recently learned there are great benefits to being a thinker, but that's another story for another day. So anyway, I think our life causes us to develop layers.

We tend to layer up to prevent similar offenses from taking place. We guard ourselves against hurts and pains, but in doing so, we don't realize it, we are retreating and morphing into something and someone we were never intended to be! I think we form these layers to shoulder the hurt if we are put in similar situations, but in doing so, we kill some of our unique selves in the process. Let's see, how do I make this plain?

Naturally, I'm quite trusting to the point of being naive. I believe the best in absolutely everyone and trust that people are genuine. I've recently had to reckon myself to the fact that in some cases, people only want to take from you. Now having learned this lesson the hard way, I am quite hesitant to develop new friendships, and I'm quite skeptical of folk who come my way. I question every one of their actions to see whether their intent is genuine or not. Pow…right there, I developed a layer. I took a little part of me and hid it under a layer of "no new friends." Now hiding under that layer is the truth: I desire camaraderie. Instead of shaking it off and just saying that was jacked up, but not everyone is like that; I threw a layer on myself to protect myself from having an episode of like kind. I've morphed into a person who doesn't trust others (I'm just being honest).

As I previously mentioned, we, though we may never admit it, are mimickers. We recreate scenarios from our childhood to do one of two things: we either respond just like our parents or we go in the absolute opposite direction. Our childhood and adulthood alike have helped shape us into the people we are today. Whether we are thriving and succeeding or sucking and lacking, if we take a gander back over our lives, we will see where we developed layers. Perhaps the layers came as a result of abuse, maybe the layers were even formed out of self-preservation. We can all give multiple excuses as to why we are all mummified and layered up, but when push comes to shove, will your excuse hold? Will it justify the fact that you're sinning daily?

You see, I've been taught the notion of spiritual simplicity. Sin is simply missing the mark. If we are not thriving and functioning as God intended for us to, guess what folks, we are *sinning*! Maybe you're not, but I am. I sin daily because I won't be true to this little nagging voice that tells me I'm great, beautiful, gifted, called, and qualified by God. I find every reason to shut it down and sit it in the corner like it is on time-out. If I were still a kid, I should be able to be the queen of hide-and-seek. I've hidden so well; I can't even find me! All I know is somewhere under all these layers, there is a *great woman of God* worthy of being found. Don't judge me; I mean, you can if it makes *you* feel better, but one thing I know is truth sets you free, and this, my friends, is my truth.

So what's left? What now? Peel back your layers. Like layers of an onion, it takes some strength to get started, may even take a nick or cut to get the process started, but once those layers start being peeled off (it takes action and work), you get to the *useful* part—the part that was intended to be added to spice up your dish. The sweet juicy part that adds flavor to your entrée. Man...this will preach, and I am so not a preacher!

You see, I'd dare say, the process of delayering may take a painful pinch, just like the nick of a knife. It may take something harsh coming your way for you to say enough is enough and start throwing off the weight of your past. Wow! Check this out. My favorite writer Paul had layered himself up as a persecutor of Christians until his painful yet amazing encounter with God. You see, he fell and looked up and had a conversation with God. He had a painful initiation into his transformation. Falling isn't easy; most of the time, you don't even look graceful when you do it, but it serves a purpose. Paul hit rock bottom and got up and went about doing his Father's business.

My friends, maybe you've hit rock bottom. Maybe you've felt the nick of a knife. Maybe something has pierced your outer layer causing you to catch glimpses of what lies beneath the surface. Glory to God! Your transformation has just started. You've had the visions; you've seen the possibilities. You know he/she is in there somewhere. Go fight for her/him. Keep working. Keep pushing; keep thriving.

Peel back one layer at a time. Tell the devil he is a liar one layer at a time. *You can do this! You are great! You are loved! God does love you!*

Man, woman, girl, boy, child, go do your work. Peel back those layers and get down to the good useful part. Get down to you! Go find the epitome of who you are and nurture yourself back to life.

Festered Grief

Okay, so this entry will undoubtedly take me out of my comfort zone to discuss some things that are quite personal but relevant to my growth.

First things first, there are two terms we need to get an understanding about: (1) fester—(a) become septic, (b) become rotten and offensive to the senses, (c) become worse or more intense, especially through long-term neglect or indifference; (2) grief—deep sorrow, especially caused by someone's death.

Let me go ahead and tell you what I want you to remember from this entry. *You have to grieve every loss you've experienced.*

To understand grief, you must understand there are different stages of grief: denial, anger, bargaining, depression, and then finally acceptance.

Now looking at the five stages, you would think grief is limited to physical loss, but I'd dare say, emotional losses should be deemed worthy of grieving as well.

It's no secret both my parents are deceased. This blog isn't about them. I've dealt with their deaths, but what I didn't deal with were remnants of the childhood I lost.

I am indeed the product of a traditional family, as both my parents were in the home, though it didn't always feel that way. There were times growing up that I felt abandoned and neglected by both parents causing me to feel unwanted, invisible, and forgotten about.

You see, I don't have those savored memories of one-on-one time with my parents, aunts, uncles, or even grandparents. I only remember being seen and not heard, seen yet not understood. I have feelings of being lonely, oh so lonely, angry, and hurt. At ten, I didn't know what to do with my feelings, so I stored them away in my emotional bank, only to ooze out into other areas of my life. It is in my earnest opinion that I didn't get the opportunity to be a child. This was a loss—a loss of innocence, a loss of formative years, and a loss of finding myself.

Fast-forward to twenty something years and here I sit typing this with tears in my eyes and pain in my heart. I'm grieving. I'm grieving the childhood I wish I had. I won't negate the good things that happened for there were some, but my truth is I didn't get what I feel I needed and deserved from my family.

This is the perfect example to talk about my festered grief. The initial shock came at ten when the little bit of attention I was getting shifted from me to my nieces and nephews, then the second shock came as my mom died when I was thirty-two. The basis was a loss, but it festered when all the feelings of losing her at ten bubbled and brewed beneath feelings of losing her at thirty-two. Twenty-two years of dealing with the loss of someone who was yet physically present. Sheesh!

I didn't realize I had compounded grief until I was chatting with my friend the other day and stumbled upon the fact that I haven't grieved my childhood. Like I said earlier, I tucked all these "feels" away in a section of my heart and wrapped it up with *caution* tape. The sad part is a portion of my heart is dedicated to harboring a twinge of hatred toward my parents because they weren't there and allowed my childhood to slip away from me. I was too young to notice, and they were too busy to pay attention.

So now that I know better, I can do better. I can choose to go ahead and cry over that ten-year-old who had to become an adult. I can admit that it wasn't fair. I can admit that it hurt me more than I was able to realize. I can do all those things, but the primary thing I have to do is move on. I have to grieve it and then leave it. So I chose today to rip off the *caution* tape, dust all the "feels" off, sit in my truth, and weep over what was lost. Though the tears fall, I must adhere to the admonition given by Paul and not weep as those who have no hope. My hope is indeed in God, and I trust, know, and wholeheartedly believe that while I can't go back and grab my childhood, I can let go of that loss and look forward to the promise of being an awesome adult!

Perhaps, you had an awesome childhood. Wonderful! I'd still dare you to check your heart for that *caution* tape. What area have you roped off because it's tender to the touch? What makes you cry when no one is looking? When you sit alone and allow your thoughts to go to that place, what is lurking and bubbling beneath the surface? That…that's the thing you need to grieve and leave. Don't just haphazardly leave it in a random place; no, take it to the cross and leave it there knowing God can restore, redeem, and reignite you.

Go and emotionally hoard no more!

Spiritual Exfoliation

So at thirty-seven, I'm beginning to have acne issues. I keep having pimples popping up, and I hate it. As a result, I've started a facial care regimen. I even purchased an exfoliating face wash *and* a hydrating facial moisturizer. Through my investigation and hypothesizing, I've reached the conclusion that I have combination skin, and as such, I'm treating it with products for folk like me whose skin can't decide if it is team oily or team dry. Man, is everything about me conflicted! I joke.

One night, as I went through my nightly routine of flipping and flopping in the bed as thoughts rapidly ran around in my mind, I thought about the purpose of the exfoliating facial wash I purchased, and of course, being the person I am, I researched it. I won't go too deep into the purpose and benefits of exfoliating because let's be honest, I'm not writing this for that reason. If you've followed me for any length of time, you'll know this will have spiritual implications.

Anyway, when we exfoliate, we use either a chemical or granular substance to rid ourselves of old skin cells to allow the new ones to shine through. According to my research, we shed old dead skin cells every thirty days. Normally, this process happens on its own without the need for assistance, but if you're like me and experience dry flaky patches, you may need to help your skin out and exfoliate. Those patches indicate the skin cells didn't shed completely. So exfoliating gives you the benefit of not having dry flaky patches, but it also does two other things that are of the utmost importance. When we exfoliate, it unclogs our pores and prevents further breakouts. Now who wouldn't want their pores unclogged if it would prevent pimple breakouts?

So here we go; let's look at this through another lens. Y'all ready? The Scripture says in Ephesians 4:22–24 "that you put off, concerning your former conduct, the old man which grows corrupt according to the deceitful lusts, and be renewed in the spirit of your mind, and that you put on the new man which was created according to God, in true righteousness and holiness."

Get it, spiritual exfoliation! At some point, you have to make a personal choice to spiritually exfoliate (my goodness, my pastor just preached a sermon on making a choice). What do I mean? You have to choose to take the Word, and allow it to wash you and remove the old dead things from the surface so that the newness that is attempting to break through can do just that!

Another scripture is 2 Corinthians 5:17 which says, "Therefore if any man be in Christ, He is a new creature; old things have passed away; behold, all things have become new." Okay, here's a quick grammar lesson. A semicolon is used when a writer could choose to end a sentence but decides to add more information. Notice there are two semicolons in the scripture. The scripture could have ended with us being new creatures, but two critical points need to be understood: (1) old things are gone, (2) *all* things have become new. Now that sounds like some exfoliating to me!

So what's my point? My point is this:

1. When we accept Christ, He becomes the tool by which we rid ourselves of our old life. He takes away the old skin cells of bad decisions, hurt, neglect, disappointment, and most importantly, He takes away the blemishes left as a result of sin.
2. When we accept the fact that we've been spiritually exfoliated, our pores are unclogged, and we are at a lower risk for a breakout. No spiritual pity party breakouts due to shame, guilt, or even despair.

Now compared to physically exfoliating, spiritual exfoliation is a decision and choice needed to be made daily! Romans 12:2 tells us to renew our minds. If I could, I'd add that this renewing of the mind needs to take place *daily*!

So here we are at the end of this text. What's the takeaway? Simply this, choose to allow Christ in to make you revitalized and anew. God can do everything *but* fail!

Prayer

Dear God, thank you for the heart you've given me. I praise you for the indwelling of the Holy Spirit. May I never forget to love you with my whole heart. Today, I declare my heart is yours to mold, shape, and use to love your people.

Amen.

Reflections

After reading Chapter 2,

___
___
___
___
___
___
___
___
___
___
___
___
___

Chapter 3

It's All about Him

> He was there before any of it came into existence and holds it all together right up to this moment.
> —Colossians 1:17 (MSG)

Limits on a Limitless God, How Dare I?

I'm at a point in my life where I just want to both know and walk in my purpose and calling. For so long, I felt teaching was it, but now I'm growing a little concerned that maybe, just maybe, I placed a limit on God and called it quits once I started teaching. Guess I had the mindset that I'd arrived. Tuh…not true. You see, walking in Christ is a journey; you never arrive until death, and considering I'm very much alive (thank you, God), I've not arrived at any designated point in my life where I can tell God I've done it all. Don't get me wrong; I enjoy teaching, but to be honest, sometimes, it's the last thing I want to do. At times, the difficulties faced in the classroom make me rethink my career choice.

What would I rather do? I'd much rather write for a living. You see, I find solace and refuge in words. They, words, comfort me when I'm disturbed, strengthen me when I'm weak, and uplift me when I'm down.

I often wonder if, based on the season of life I'm in, my life's purpose shifts. Perhaps I am meant to teach, but what if it is no longer in a classroom setting. How do I tie writing into teaching? I don't publicize it, but I truly feel that I'm meant to be a writer. Some people have come alongside me and suggested the same. I believe they were sent as confirmation from God.

At times, I become frustrated because of the pressures placed on teachers to perform miracles. I'm upset when my kids don't perform well on tests. I'm bothered when behavior is an issue. See how none of these emotions are happy ones? I'm bothered. I know and fully believe when we are in the will of God, better emotions become companions as we walk that journey.

When I sit and think about all that I can do instead of teaching, I become bogged down because my degrees are in education. Seems there is nothing else I can do…then a startling revelation hits me…in and of myself, there is absolutely nothing else I can do. I place limits on God when I simply resign myself to being limited to education. He is the greatest there ever was and ever will be. It's crazy how one of my favorite scriptures can be tied into this. "Now, unto Him who *is* able to do exceedingly abundantly above all we can ask or think according to the power that worketh in us" (Ephesians 3:20). You see, it's His power that works in us. Even though I get frustrated with what appears to be a lack of progress in my students, it's still His power that is working in me to teach those children. Though my writing is nowhere near where I want it to be, it's His power that works in me to write.

If (since) I rely on God's power, who am I to say what can't happen with my writing? How dare I place limits on a limitless God! In my mind, I'll one day have a blog that people subscribe to and make my living doing that. This is what I think and imagine. If the Word says He can do *more than that*, why then do I limit myself to blogging occasionally when I have time? Why not blog daily like it's already how I make my living? If I were in court right now, I'd be found guilty of placing limits on God.

Don't think this is only about me! If you check your life, I'm certain you've placed limits on God in some way yourself. Think about that area that when you think about it, you just say, "Oh, that's just how it has and probably always will be." No, ma'am…no, sir!

There is no settling in God. He is an ever progressing and moving God. He has the greatest things in store for us.

Dare yourself to stop placing limits on God. Think about your current position in life, then think about this scripture...1 Corinthians 2:9 says, "Eye has not seen, nor ear heard, nor have entered into the heart of man the things which God has prepared for those who love Him."

God only has great things in store for us. Trust Him to do exceedingly, abundantly, above... He simply cannot fail!

The Nerve

> Therefore if the Son makes you free, you shall be free indeed. (John 8:36)

> Stand fast therefore in the liberty by which Christ has made us free, and do not be entangled again with a yoke of bondage. (Galatians 5:1)

Let me go ahead and get to the punch line of this story. God has, through the amazing sacrifice of His Son, Christ, liberated us and set us free to live an abundant life, but we, in our finite thinking and lack of understanding, live a restricted life of narrow thinking.

So let's backtrack; reading the verses of scripture above *should* make you think and wonder about your life. Are you truly liberated, or is it just something you say to pump yourself up? Do you live a life free from bondage, or do you simply step out of your cell, put on a performance, then go home and lock yourself back up? These are real questions! They require self-reflection and what is commonly known as a gut check. Do you? Do I? As a matter of fact, I do! Even as I am typing this, certain performance antics I use are coming to mind.

On the outside, I smile; I laugh. I crack jokes, and if I'm feeling daring, I just might dance. Oh, but when I get home, that's when I ever so gently put my handcuffs back on and go sit in my little solitary confined cell.

It's while I'm in this cell that the negative self-talk begins. It's in this cell that I berate and belittle myself, thinking of myself as inferior to others. It's in this cell that I realize I've been spinning my wheels. It is while I'm in this cell that I feel like I don't matter, and others simply tolerate me because it's the "nice" thing to do. My cell gives me a warped depiction of my life and limits me to living a life that is in direct contrast to the life Christ envisioned for me as He hung on that cross.

As with anything in life, the best way to refuse to succumb to life's issues or problems is to stand and face them. Know in facing them, you aren't alone. I've been taught to face issues using the Word, hence the scriptures at the beginning of this entry. Let's revisit them:

1. John 8:36 tells us that when Christ freed us, He freed us forever! So let's put this in perspective. At one point in time, I typed a spiritual resignation letter. When I resigned, I applied this scripture and said it was enough with living a life that God hadn't called me to live. I took a giant step, but I kind of sort of stepped back a bit and allowed myself to start thinking thoughts like I was still in that position, which is where the second passage of scripture comes in.
2. Galatians 5:1, when I sit and think about it, it encourages me to stay away from all previous positions that weren't in line with God's will for my life. Since I've been freed, I simply can't afford to go backward and pick up memoirs of things of the past. I, on the other hand, must continue to press forward. Like Paul, I have to forget the things that are behind me and press toward the mark of the high call of Christ.

When combined (which the Bible doesn't do…this is an Anitra-ism), those scriptures, when I think about them, sound like this. *Okay, so, Anitra, I've freed you, set you free; this is a promise I'm upholding. Nothing can stop you but you. Remember you are free, and whatever you do, don't go picking up things from the past that can cause you to revert to an imprisoned life.*

Parents, can you imagine saying these words to your child/children only for them to walk away and go place themselves back in both handcuffs and solitary confinement? The nerve, right!

Well, God is our Father, and we do it. The nerve of us! We sit Sunday after Sunday, Wednesday after Wednesday, and listen to a *rhema* Word from God. We shout while the Word is going forth, jumping to our feet as our pastor illuminates the Word. Saying amen aloud, scribbling notes, the tearing up of eyes, the sorrowful weeping, we do all of that, but when no one is looking and we are left alone, what do some of us do? We go back and buy into the lies of the enemy and decide within ourselves that God has to be overreaching and thinking of someone else. Surely, His Word doesn't apply to us! The nerve!

Who are we to call God a liar? What? That's what we do when we simply cannot imagine His word applying to our lives. We call Him a liar when we place ourselves back in bondage. Reverting to bondage is *not* something God would do. The whole aim of Christ's coming was to grant us a relationship with God, which encompasses an abundant life. Bondage and abundance are antonyms. They simply *cannot and will not coexist*! How dare we work up the unmitigated gall to do this to God. It's like we are spitting in His face and saying His promises are null and void. The nerve!

A holy God made promises thousands of years before our existence, and now suddenly, we are so bad that He changes His mind? Aw naw…not possible. You see, the amount of love God has for us can never change. We can't make Him love us any more or less than He already does. It's this love that enables us to live a life free from bondage. Take into consideration that both of the scriptures for this text revolve around the actions Christ took. It was in His death that we were made alive! The nerve of us to walk around like the walking dead—heads bowed, hearts broken, and minds warped. No! That is not an abundant life!

You know, we have some nerve living a life that is so far beneath the dreams and goals God has for us. I can only think and attribute this to a lack of trust. Because we've been abused and misguided by people, our first instinct is to doubt first, trust later. While this idea may work with people, it simply does not work with God. Just as bondage and abundance can't coexist neither can faith and doubt.

For every positive, there is a negative. It's time for us to take a stand and choose the positive. Choose to see the best in yourself even at times when you look or feel the worst. Look at your life and find all the silver linings you can. Search your problems for promise. Dig deep and discover determination where desperation used to exist. Turn all your crappy situations and problems into manure and grow from them.

You see, I don't write this as an individual who has it all figured out; no, I write this as someone who is writing out a truth that she just discovered. As always, if my journey to self-discovery can help someone else, it's worth it. It's no secret I'll be forty in a few years. My prayer is that I have all this worked out by then. Far too many years have passed with me accepting the enemy's lies and whispers as truth. No, God has called me to a beautiful life, and I'm tired of simply existing. I want to live and live abundantly. We should all work up the nerve to be the person God loves and sacrificed His Son for.

We should work up the nerve and passionately pursue and live in all the promises God has made to each of us. That's what we should have the nerve to do!

Safe in His Arms

Today, I sat and listened to *"Safe in His Arms,"* and I feel as though this is the first time I've ever really *heard* the song and internalized the message therein. The lyrics are fairly simple and are based on the twenty-third Psalm which is a well-known and often-quoted passage of Scripture. I've heard the twenty-third Psalm time and time again, but today as I listened to the song, I went back and read the twenty-third Psalm, and it made so much more sense.

The first words of the twenty-third Psalm are, "The Lord is my shepherd; I shall not want." The first words of the song are, "Because the Lord is my shepherd, I shall not want." (Unfortunately, I'm about to get all technical and delve into my teacher mindset.) Both of those sentences are complex sentences; one uses the conjunction *because;*

comparatively, the other uses a semicolon. One of the purpose of a semicolon is to stand in the place of a conjunction, so again, both sentences are complex, having one independent clause and one dependent clause. While they both express the same thought and are centered around the same topic, I am more inspired by the biblical version of this statement. Why? Because in that sentence, the second portion is *dependent* upon the first… Watch…

The Lord is my shepherd; I shall not want.

The independent clause, "The Lord is my shepherd," is independent because it can stand alone; it expresses a complete thought. However, the second portion, "I shall not want," is *completely* dependent upon the first clause. If I were to simply walk up to someone and say, I shall not want. I'm certain they would have a rather perplexing expression on their face and become curious as to what it is I am trying to convey, *but* if I walk up to someone and say, the Lord is my shepherd; there's not much else I need to explain for them to understand my statement.

Some time ago, I learned the importance of the relationship between shepherd and sheep. I was told that oftentimes, shepherds would carry their sheep so that the sheep would know the shepherd's voice. I was also told that sheep don't always know what is best for them and can become so engrossed in grazing that a cliff can easily cause their demise because they would simply continue grazing unaware of the cliff.

Sometimes, we stay in a situation unaware of the fact that holding on to something God wants to deliver us from can ultimately lead to our death spiritually and/or physically. If we didn't have a shepherd who knows better than we do, our lives would undoubtedly be vicious cycles of bad decisions. While it is easy to focus on the positive aspects of having a shepherd look out for you, we must remain mindful of the fact that sometimes we have to be broken to be rebuilt.

It is said that a sheep that wanders and roams away from its shepherd has to have its leg broken to be taught to stay with its shepherd. After the sheep's leg is broken, the shepherd takes his time and tends to the sheep all the while talking to it so that the sheep learns the importance of not straying away from its shepherd's voice. I was that sheep that wandered, that sheep who got so far away that all I could hear was the faint whisper of a familiar voice, but thanks be to God I was brought back into the fold.

Previously, I've mentioned how my life is being rebuilt and how I'm having to start over, but today, I'm going to be completely transparent because let's face it, this life I live is so not about me. Back on June 17, 2014, I sat in my living room and watched my car be repossessed. I did nothing to stop it because there wasn't anything I could do. I didn't realize it then, but that was the beginning of me resting in God. Throwing my hands up and saying Lord, I *still* trust you in this situation was the biggest step I could ever really take. I used to have such a *huge* issue surrendering, and I didn't even know it. I figured if I weren't doing it, it wouldn't get done. If it needed to be fixed, it was up to me. Yeah…that was amazingly unsuccessful.

So six years ago, I surrendered to God, and I can honestly say, I don't regret it at all. Oh, how I've come to know God in a much more personal way. I'd heard people say things to describe the positive attributes of God but lacked a personal connection to those things. I'd heard Him called a way maker, but now I know He is because there hasn't been *one* major thing I missed due to transportation issues; no, not one! You see, the Lord is my shepherd; I shall not want. It is because I acknowledge that He is my shepherd—the one responsible for feeding me, clothing me, protecting me, disciplining me, and loving me—that I find safety in His arms. I needn't be afraid of anything because the Lord is my shepherd.

Earlier, I talked about the independent clause and the dependent clause. In my relationship with God, I'm most certainly the dependent clause. I'm completely dependent upon Him for *everything*. He can do whatever He pleases with or without me; however, I am amazingly limited without Him. Having to lose things has certainly put me in a great position to gain. While I have to admit there was a time when I was so far outside of the will of God that I couldn't hear his voice, I can now say, that's no longer the case. I hear my God when He speaks, and that means more to me than any of the things I've lost. Being able to hear His voice consistently simply means I'm right where I need to be. I'm well within His will. I'm walking with Him beside me daily; simply put, I'm *safe* in *His* arms.

You Keep on Keeping Me

One of my all-time favorite gospel songs to sing is "Safe in His Arms." Can you imagine how excited I was when I fell in love with another song that mentioned being safe in the arms of our Lord? Not only does this song speak of God's ability to cover and protect us, but it goes on to talk about how God keeps us.

The song, found on Travis Greene's album *The Hill*, is entitled "You Keep Me," but as they sing the song, they use the phrase "You keep on keeping me" to give an extra reason to shout like one is needed; they add that He keeps on keeping us over and over again (I love to sing the woman's part of this toward the end).

Let me backtrack and just talk about the beginning of the song. Travis begins the song by saying, "I've sinned, fell short of your glory, messed up, ain't proud of it, but your love is more than enough. You keep on keeping me." Isn't this the story of our lives? We mess up; we sin time and time again, *but* God keeps on keeping us! Isn't that a *perfect* depiction of love? Who would continue to love and keep someone over and over despite their sins? Only God! What love that the all-knowing, all-powerful God continues to keep us knowing that we are prone to sin, knowing that we are imperfect, flawed, selfish, fleshly people! Man, that excites me. Maybe you've lived a perfect life, I sure have not! My life, my decisions haven't always reflected my knowledge of and personal relationship with Christ, *but* He keeps on keeping me safe in His arms!

As I have listened to this song all day long, I found it interesting that Travis didn't just say you keep me but used the word keeping too. Of course, me being who I am, I sat and thought about this for a minute, and then my inner nerd kicked in, and I had a light bulb moment.

To keep means to hold or retain in one's possession, to hold as one's own. Powerful, right? Wait for it. Keeping is the present participle of the word keep which means it is *continuous* and unending.

So if you put it all together, God continuously, without fail, holds us as His own over and over; every time we sin, He forgives us. Our position in Him isn't thrown out or canceled because of our sin; no, over and over He retains us, holds us as His own.

I knew I loved this song as soon as I heard it; it's been on repeat for at least a week now. What can I say? When I like a song, *I really like* it, but I guess it's more than just liking it; it's the fact that the song ministers to me.

I can sit and reflect on my life and get stuck thinking about the times I failed God—the times where I knowingly and deliberately chose sin, the times when I ignored God and did what I wanted to because I was grown and didn't need to follow Muh's (my mother) warnings and threats (she didn't play). I know there have been times when I have abused grace: going into sin with my eyes wide open, depending on grace to keep me from experiencing God's wrath. Even in that, God keeps on keeping me. He didn't look at me and deem me unworthy.

Perhaps you're currently in a vicious cycle of sinning. You looked up and realized you are so far away from God it isn't even funny. You're having that moment where nothing you're around looks familiar. You've found yourself in a place where you never imagined you'd be. Your sin has carried you farther than you ever meant to go, and you've stayed there longer than you planned on. You feel disconnected, abandoned, and too far away from God for Him to hear your cries. Lies, I tell you! All lies straight from the pit of hell. God has kept on keeping you! Nothing you've done has been so bad that He chose just you to abandon. No, oh, how He loves you! Trust me, if I shared just a bit of my past, you'd be surprised! Just know, I was out there too, did a bunch of stuff I'm not proud of, *but* even in that, God kept me. I am yet here all because of His grace and love and that same grace and love are available for you! God is no respecter of person; He did it for me, and He'll do it for you too. All you have to do is accept Him as your personal Lord and Savior. Believe that Jesus was born and died for your sins.

> For God so greatly loved and dearly prized the world that He [even] gave up His only begotten [unique] Son, so that whoever believes in [trusts in, clings to relies on] Him, shall not perish [come to destruction, be lost] but have [everlasting] life. (John 3:16 AMP)
>
> Because if you acknowledge and confess with your lips that Jesus is Lord and in your heart believe [adhere to, trust in, and rely on the truth] that God raised Him from the dead, you will be saved. For with the heart, a person believes [adheres to, trusts in, and relies on Christ] and so is justified [declared righteous, acceptable to God], and with the mouth, he confesses [declares openly and speaks out freely his faith] and confirms [his] salvation. (Romans 10:9–10 AMP)

Won't you trust God to "keep on keeping you over and over"? It'll be the best decision of your life! Take it from me.

Trust in Him

There are several promises in the Bible that are all dependent upon our willingness to believe and trust in God's ability to keep His promises. To believe something is to trust in it, and to trust in something is to hold fast to it and depend on it to be reliable and trust in its ability to perform as promised.

Proverbs 3:5–6 illuminates not only the power of God but the power of one of His promises. The scripture first gives us a progression of steps we must take then anchors it with a promise from God.

- Trust in Lord with all your heart: Trusting in God is esteeming or affirming Him to be who He says and has proven Himself to be. Think about the most awesome thing God has done for you. Now reflect on His awesome wonders we get the privilege of reading about in His Word. All of His actions stem from love. How do I know? He loves us so much He sent His Son to die for us and pay the ransom He set. He established that the wages of sin is death, but it was a death we didn't have to pay. His Son paid the ransom in full, one time and for all. He is *that God*; what's not to trust? He doesn't want us to put part of our trust in Him and the other part in worldly things or even ourselves. His direct instructions are to trust in God with the whole of our heart, which means every ounce of our being, even the hidden parts of our psyche and personalities, even the minuscule and finite pieces of who we are. The essence of who we are must put trust in God. After we put our full trust in Him being who He says He is, we are to lean not to our understanding.

- Lean not to your own understanding: Only once we have put our full and complete trust in God does it become easy to lean not to our own understanding. When we look at who He is and how He functions, we realize we know nothing at all. We are completely ignorant of how we are to live our lives. He has our entire being planned—the trials, tribulations, and even mistakes. How dare we attempt to lean to our understanding. When we lean too hard on our own understanding, that's exactly when we fall. Examples of leaning to our understanding could be as simple as hearing God's voice and deciding you know a better way to accomplish the task. We lean to our own understanding when we fail to consult God before doing something or deciding. Our understanding pales in comparison to the thoughts of God. He is an omniscient and omnipresent God; how dare we try to figure things out on our own. It would be foolish for us to do that, but when we make moves without consulting God, that's exactly what we are doing: leaning to our own understanding. This is in direct opposition to what God would have us do. We are told to trust in Him, not lean to our own understanding, then we are asked to acknowledge Him in all our ways.

- In all your ways acknowledge Him: I must point out that this portion of the scripture follows a semicolon. The purpose of a semicolon is to continue a thought that the author could have ended. Instead of leaving us hanging with not leaning to our understanding, we are told exactly what to do when we don't lean to our understanding. So let's recap. "Trust in God with all your heart and lean not to your own understanding; in all your ways acknowledge Him." What does it mean to acknowledge God? To acknowledge is to admit the truth. By now you should notice a cyclical thought. The scripture began with trusting in God, and here we are with a command about trusting Him. In essence, this portion of the scripture could read, in all your ways, admit the truth of who He is. Basically, in everything you do, admit the truth of who He is. Guaranteed, this will prevent many of the mistakes we make. Walking daily with the conscious decision to admit the truth of who He is will have us in a constant state of praise and worship as we see His hand at work in our day-to-day situations and circumstances; however, this only comes if we acknowledge Him in all our ways. Again, this Scripture is a progression of steps. Once we have completed the steps—trusting in Him, leaning not to our own understanding, and acknowledging Him—we are then given a promise! How exciting!
- He shall direct your paths: I love the word shall. Shall isn't a conditional word. Whatever comes after it is something you can stand on; it's a promise! He *shall* direct your paths. When something is directed, it is guided to make it to a specific destination or according to plan. As we know, according to Jeremiah 29:11, God knows the plans He has for us, plans of peace to prosper us, not harm us but to bring us to an expected end. Notice the phrase expected end, it's another indication that God has already planned

our lives. He's just waiting for us to surrender and follow the path He is directing.

Whenever I have to go to a new destination, I type it into my GPS. The actual progression of events should be the following:

1. Trusting in the GPS
2. Leaning not to my own understanding
3. Acknowledging the GPS with every turn I make
4. Allowing the GPS to direct my path

Just as in our spiritual walk, we often mess up around step 2; we begin thinking we know more and better than the GPS and make our own decisions, turns, choice of roads, etc. Ultimately, we add a delay in reaching our destination. This could be a result of getting lost or taking a route that is longer than the one originally planned by the GPS. How true of our journey with Christ. We trust in Him as long as we are on familiar territory, but when we traverse to a distant unfamiliar land, we want to retreat to that which is familiar and comfortable and end up adding time to our journey. We only hinder God when we don't follow the progression of steps given to us.

The amazing truth that we tend to forget is that we also have the promise that God's Word won't return to Him void (Isaiah 55:11). In this verse, Proverbs 3:5–6, we receive what could be considered a conditional promise; it is contingent upon us holding up our end, following the progression of events. If we trust in Him, lean not to our own understanding, acknowledge Him in *all* our ways, then and only then will He direct our paths. Trust God; don't lean to your own understanding. Acknowledge Him in everything you do and watch Him direct your path!

That's Love

Lately, I've caught myself thinking about dating and marriage a *lot*. Like I have to actually reel my thoughts back in. I promise I said I wanted to take some time to just be by myself and learn how to absolutely love myself, but the itch to date again is becoming more prevalent. Sigh… My most recent past relationships were a *trip*, but they taught me something. I won't dare delve into details to protect the guilty (they certainly weren't innocent), but let's suffice it to say, I learned what nonexamples of love look like. Reflecting on two previous relationships, I'll admit when both of these relationships ended, of course, I had mixed feelings. I was broken up with in one, and the other, I ended the relationship. I won't lie; my heart ached more when I was broken up with than when I ended things. That was the *first* time I'd ever been broken up with! I digress; the point is, I thought both individuals loved me but came to the realization, the harsh realization that they didn't.

The teacher in me knows when you fully understand something, you can identify its true characteristics and eliminate the characteristics that don't fit. To do this, though, you have to be exposed to both then use your analytical skills and background knowledge to do the comparison. Now let's break down background knowledge. If you were in my reading class, we'd discuss making inferences right here, but since we aren't, I'll just keep it moving.

Background knowledge is formed through life experiences: good, bad, and indifferent. It is established from childhood and extends well into adulthood. It comes by way of lessons learned, attempted feats, victories, and failures. It encompasses wisdom, knowledge, and even common sense. It is also known as the essence of your worldview or how you view the world. Can you see where I'm going? Yes, we all have background knowledge when it comes to love, whether we are in love, have been in love, or are simply waiting to fall in love; we all have an idea and belief in how it should be.

Well, my initial idea of love was butterflies, shooting stars, romantic glances, hand-holding, cuddling, you know, all the mushy stuff most girls want. While these things can and may be indicative of love, there's a better guideline for love. All the aforementioned characteristics can be considered outward expression of an inner love but can also simply be manners by which to spend time with someone. Do these things truly indicate love? I'm sorry, but no. Having been married before, I've experienced these things and didn't bit more have love one for another than a toaster for a piece of toast.

So what is love? First, love is an action word. It compels you to act on behalf of someone else to better their condition or life. It's selfless, sacrificial, unconditional, and ever giving. It doesn't run out, isn't superficial, and most importantly doesn't hold grudges or look for a payout. Christ is the perfect example of this love. There is a gospel song that I genuinely love, "No Greater Love." The chorus is simply,

> Jesus went to Calvary
> To save a wretch,
> Like you and me;
> That's love, that's love.
>
> They hung Him high,
> They stretched Him wide.
> He hung His head, for me He died;
> That's love, that's love.
>
> That's not how the story ends,
> Three days later He rose again;
> That's love, that's love.

That! That is love in his most genuine and pure form. Selfless, Jesus went to Calvary. Sacrificial, He hung His head; for me, He died. Yes, *this*, this is the perfect example of love. Love is so powerful! This love is teaching me to wait for the one God has for me. To wait until He sends my king who first and foremost understands this love, trusts, and believes in our God who demonstrated this love while we were yet sinners, and finally, that man who knows how to love himself so that he may love others.

We all know everything in a believer's life works out for their good, right? Initially, I didn't see any good thing coming out of those situations; however, God allowed me to see what love isn't so that I could appreciate His love.

Prayer

Dear God, thank you for being the beginning and the end, Alpha and Omega, King of kings, and Lord of lords. I acknowledge that without you, there would be nothing in this world. I praise you for everything that you've created. Thank you for speaking this world and my existence into being. Let me never take this world nor my life for granted.

Amen.

Reflections

After reading Chapter 3,

_____
_____
_____
_____
_____
_____
_____
_____
_____
_____
_____
_____
_____
_____

Chapter 4

In Him

> In Him we live and move and have our being.
> —Acts 17:28a (NKJV)

Live in the Grace

During Wednesday night service, my pastor made a statement that truly resounded deep within me. He simply said, "Remember, God has graced you to deal with your issues. Live in the grace." Ironically, my name means God's grace...perhaps that is why I could identify with this statement.

Once I made it home, I had time to meditate on the statement and just examine what it meant to me and how I could apply it to my life. I started by thinking about the word live.

To live is to decide to do what is necessary to sustain life. We live by way of careers, businesses, and jobs, but ultimately, we make the choice to live, and we make this choice daily. Daily, we get out of bed and decide to go to work, make phone calls, achieve our goals, etc. Without choosing to comply with daily living responsibilities, our lives would undoubtedly stop. Now that we've examined the word live, let's take a look at the word grace.

Grace, when explained by most biblical teachers, pastors, and preachers, is *God's Riches At Christ's Expense*. The more sophisticated definition of grace is an act of kindness. You see grace is getting what we don't deserve.

Based on what my pastor was teaching, living in grace is not something you can do subconsciously as choosing to live in grace is just that—a choice. It is a deliberate decision that one makes each day, quite possibly, even multiple times a day. As we know, our lives are filled with choices, obstacles, decisions, problems, etc. We choose to live in grace when we, first, face the problems, and second, choose to remind ourselves to *abound* in grace.

Abounding in grace simply means to have an overflow of grace. Now this grace isn't to be confused with us extending kindness to others; no, it is the portion of grace God has given each of us. Let me pause and say everyone's portion of grace will be different as it is based on your faith. Okay, let's see if I can make this make a little more sense. When we choose to live in grace, we're telling our problems they aren't insurmountable. We're telling our situations they aren't dead ends. We're telling our obstacles they aren't roadblocks, just detours. When we choose to live in grace, we make the conscious decision to use the shed blood of Christ to defeat anything that seeks to rise and make it seem like it is greater than the sacrifice Jesus made on the cross.

Living in grace is taking the message of the cross that death, hell, and the grave are defeated and facing life's tough times.

What will you do the next time you are faced with an obstacle or tough decision? Will you tuck your tail, run, and hide, or will you live in grace and face the issue dead-on?

Victory in Failure

The past couple of years of my life have undoubtedly been chaotic and tumultuous. So much so that it made me doubt my sanity, literally. Experiencing panic attacks, anxiety attacks, migraines, pre-diabetic/diabetic issues, hypertension, polycystic ovarian syndrome, and many other things took its toll. Add to that a truly unhealthy marriage and the repercussions of that and I think anyone would be a wee bit fragile. While the aforementioned things are certainly worthy of attention and concern, I'm now at a point in my life where I can truly recognize the cause of all of these things. You see, the sicknesses, depression, anxiety, etc. are cataclysmic of a life outside of the will of God. Today, I look and reflect on my life and one word comes to mind: failure. I admit it; I have failed, and yes, it hurts.

Since I can remember, I've lived my life with such a heightened fear of failure that it literally became a stronghold. Avoiding germs, risky behaviors (somewhat), dangerous places, dangerous people, and always being serious in my endeavors, I thought I was safe; I thought I'd arrived. I thought I'd finally shaken hands with this mystery known as adulthood. All in all, I thought I'd prepared myself for a wonderful life. I was right. I had prepared myself for a wonderful life. I wouldn't dare allow myself to be involved with anything that was outside of my realm of control. I wouldn't live by faith. This is where I failed. I planned my life according to what I wanted to do, according to my personal desires, and more importantly, according to my limited understanding. This choice is in direct opposition to what the Lord commands of us. He tells us in His Word to trust in Him and not lean unto our understanding. So why did I make the choice to begin to live my life according to my very own "gospel"? I misunderstood the simple things of my spiritual life; I misunderstood faith, trusting in God, and more importantly, I misunderstood and took advantage of God's will for my life.

Myles Munroe is often quoted as saying, "When the purpose of a thing is misunderstood, abuse is inevitable." Failing to understand what it meant to be in the will of God, to trust Him, to have faith in Him and His Word, I rebelled, thereby causing me to abuse His love for me. I figured if I didn't pay my tithes, God would just look the other way. I figured if I shacked (yep...I'm a reformed shacker), God wouldn't mind; we were already being intimate, so what was the difference? So yeah, I'm familiar with fornication. Oh...don't turn up your nose at me; at least, I'm honest enough to call out *some* of my sins. It was a slippery slope from then on. I pretty much set a flimsy set of parameters for myself and excused myself to indulge in the sins within those parameters. I mean, as long as I wasn't murdering people, robbing banks, or kidnapping children, I was good, right?

Wrong. Let us be reminded that no sin is greater than the next; it all stinks in the nostrils of God. While trying to maintain a safety net around me, I rebelled, and I *failed*.

Today, I sit and I'm dealing with major consequences of my choice to live outside of the will of God, and I've confessed unto God that I failed. Outside of His will, He has yet protected me as no major harm or danger came upon me, *but* His favor hasn't been ever-present as it should be. Just being honest, my finances aren't *anywhere* near where they need to be, and I once again, refusing to fail, quit paying my tithes to make accommodations for other things in my life—again, outside of the will of God.

I started this post off with the title "Victory in Failure," and here's the point:

I lived my life according to my definitions, ideas, theories, practices; I kept fixing things myself and never once did I allow God to do anything. I kept Him limited, and as a result, I failed; oh, but I'm coming to realize just how much victory there is in failure. I serve an omnipotent and omniscient God who, according to His Word, simply *cannot* fail. I failed because I was doing everything on my own. I wasn't seeking first His kingdom, and as such, "all things" couldn't be added unto me. So I admit it; I failed, and yes, my emotions are involved, but I am finding peace in knowing that right when I've failed, God can then begin to work. So really, there is only victory in failure.

Now that I have tried it on my own and failed, I've moved out of the way, and God can now begin to do just what He said He would do: provide, defend, bless, increase, and protect. Wouldn't that be considered as a victory? I'd say so. I'm at the point where I've hit rock bottom, and I'm glad about it. I'm at a point in my life I'd never thought I'd be. I'd never thought that I, Anitra Lachelle Freeney, MEd would be struggling financially. I never thought that I'd come home to no electricity (I do have power again). I never thought that I'd be experiencing so many disconnection notices, etc. Seriously, I graduated salutatorian from high school, cum laude from DBU with my BA in elementary education, and then again with a 4.0 GPA from DBU with my MEd in reading and English as second language. Oh…I have letters behind my name; I have a five-figure income, and I'm *still* struggling. It's only because *I'm* doing it. I quit. I can't continue on this path as it is not working for me. The way I like to think of it is about my vision and the limitations therein.

Unfortunately, I inherited vision from my mother in my left eye (I'm farsighted) and from my father in my right eye (I'm nearsighted). Yeah…jacked up vision I have. Within this vision debacle, my peripheral vision lacks, and there's only a certain distance I can see, especially while driving at night. My vision is limited, so if someone is privileged enough to be my passenger, I often ask them what the signs say, etc. because I recognize my limitations. That's where I am in life. I've told the Lord I surrender because I can only see to a certain point, but He has limitless vision, and He's already planned out my life. I don't have to strain to attempt to see down the road; all I have to do is trust Him that I won't hit a curb. I won't miss my exit. I won't go the wrong way on a dangerous road, and most importantly, I won't get lost and end up in a foreign place with no help. All I have to do is crank the car, put it in gear, and allow Him to navigate me on this journey. With someone telling you every little hidden bump, pothole, twist, and turn on the road, how can you lose? You can't. It is impossible to fail when/if God is the head of your life.

Failure is imminent when we live our lives according to our fleshly desires, but right when you fail, God is there to turn it around and extend to you the victory that was granted when Christ died on the cross.

So, my friends, I've failed, but I praise God, for He is granting me victory.

Trust me; there's only victory in failure. Remember this text because one day soon, I will be able to write and tell the great extent of victory that God is granting me. I don't have the physical manifestation of it yet, but I'm trusting God that He will do just what needs to be done.

Bound

So I decided to unlock my locs, and I did it! It took a *very* long time (most of my Christmas break), but I did it. Of course, God showed me a lesson after I'd finished with the project.

I'd had my locs for four years, and I rocked them…or at least I think I did. During these four years, my hair became comfortable and grew tremendously. At one point, I'd decided to not ever cut them and let them grow as long as they possibly could; I changed my mind.

So here it is; just months after my four-year locversary, and I'd decided to take them down. I was so nervous about the process, but I knew it was something I greatly desired, so I sat and armed with a very large bottle of conditioner, water, and a rattail comb combed out every loc on my head (I intended to count them, but I quickly lost count).

Once I finished combing them out, I was left with hair thicker and healthier than it was when I locked my hair! I was and still am impressed! Now the hard part is getting my hair to do something other than being an Afro puff (yes, I'm currently rocking an afro puff). You see, my hair had been bound for four years and now that it is experiencing foreign freedom, it doesn't know what to do with itself. It thinks it still needs to be tangled and matted, but that's not true. It, my hair, now has the full potential to flow freely and heck, blow in the wind if it should so desire, but it needs to realize every strand is freed from the tangles that once held it bound!

Can you see where I'm going? At times in our lives, we find ourselves comfortable in bondage because it's been a part of our lives for so long. At my church, there is a common phrase that we use. It has to do with people walking out of comfort zones in search and pursuit of the greater than on the other side. We like to say people get so comfortable in their familiar bondage that they can't accept their foreign freedom! Man, every time I hear that saying, it does something to me.

Like my hair, maybe you've been bound for years. You have found yourself in the same situation so many times, you just don't know what to do. Bondage stifles your growth and limits your potential until you, with the help of the Lord, break out of it and embrace your foreign freedom. You see, deciding to free my hair was quite easy and natural. I just sat and decided. Starting the process was easy but following through and seeing the task to completion, allowing my hair to be completely free, was one of the most difficult tasks I've had to complete in my life! I wanted the outcome to come quickly, but I had to tarry with my hair for roughly eleven to twelve days doing nothing but combing out each loc individually.

In life, we can set our sights on the glorious vision of freedom. We can decide to pray and ask God for deliverance, which we know He will undoubtedly grant; however, walking the walk until your deliverance is complete, yeah, that's the hard part. Choosing daily to live as though you are delivered even in the face of the situation that has caused you to be bound, yeah, that's seeing that thing through until it is brought to fruition.

That walk between bound and free can be likened unto the journey Abraham took Isaac on. He didn't know exactly how the task would end; he wasn't exactly sure of how God was going to move nor did he honestly know if God would spare his son's life, but he *trusted God* fully and completely without reservation.

While on your deliverance journey, you must continue; you have to persevere! Paul tells us in Philippians 3:13–14 that he doesn't count himself to have attained, but he *does* forget what's in the past and *presses* toward what yet lies ahead. We must do this very thing.

While taking down my hair, I couldn't keep reflecting on the styles I used to wear with the locs; no, I had to keep focusing on what I wanted out of the task. I had to keep my mind focused on the result that I desired: free-flowing natural hair.

What about this bondage versus freedom? Glad you asked. The most amazing thing about God is the fact that He has already worked out everything we need in our lives. He has our whole life planned out by His purpose and plan for our lives. We pray and ask for things and breakthroughs as we see fit, but He has already granted them. We simply have to walk the walk of faith and trust that He will bring us through.

When I took down my very last loc, it was on a Monday, January 8, 2018, at one thirty in the morning! I had resorted to tears, as I was exhausted, but I didn't give up; no, I believed the outcome would be worth all the work I'd put in. What am I trying to say? I'm saying, trust God; trust the process. He can't fail, and He won't leave you. As a matter of fact, He promises *never* to leave us nor forsake us.

The Reason and Result

Okay, the secret is out: I'm a teacher (insert sarcastic gasp). No, seriously, as a teacher, you never stop learning. This week as I taught text structures, one of the structures in a nonfiction text is cause and effect. As I introduced cause and effect, I used my own teaching words and gave the kids the following thinking stems: The cause is the reason why something happened. The effect is what happened. Out of nowhere, one of my kids raised her hand and said, "Oh, I get it. The cause is the reason, and the effect is the result." My kids know I like to teach using alliteration so that the words I use stick in their memory. I was undoubtedly impressed with my dear child's revelation, and it actually stuck with me. As a matter of fact, I taught the rest of my classes using her words. Now I had no idea her words would transcend class and be used by God to remind me of the basis of the Gospel.

John 3:16 says, "For God so loved the world that He gave His only begotten Son that whosoever believes in Him shall not perish, but have everlasting life." The word *for* is used but could easily be substituted with the word *because*. Because God so loved the world He gave His only begotten Son that whosoever believes in Him shall not perish but have everlasting life. When we take the time to look at this verse in this context, we can see the cause and effect or the reason and the result.

> Cause (reason)—God so loved the world.
> Effect (result)—He gave His only Son.
> Watch this; the effect becomes a cause.
> Cause (reason)—He gave His only Son.

> Effect (result)—Whosoever believes in Him shall not perish but have everlasting life.

What's the point? I'm glad you asked. The point is simply that the Bible is one giant book of promises that are all cause-and-effect statements. Think I'm kidding? Look at John 10:10—in this verse, Jesus is describing how the enemy is nothing but a thief. He compares Himself to the enemy explaining why He came, then He hits us with another cause and effect relationship. In part B of verse 10, He says, "I am come that they may have life and have it more abundantly." Here we go…

> Cause (reason)—I am come.
> Effect (result)—That they might have life and have it more abundantly.

What is the point of this text? The point is simply to share a realization I had through teaching my kids. If Christ hadn't come and died, there'd simply be no positive effects on our lives. The catalyst of all the promises of God is based on the fact that Christ came and served as the atonement for our sins.

One more point and I'm done.

This past Sunday, our Sunday school lesson was comparing the old covenant with the new covenant. Basically, in a nutshell, here is what I gleaned from our lesson. Because Christ came, we now have access to our heavenly Father for ourselves; no one needs to go in on our behalf. We now have the promise of a liberated and bountiful life. That, once again, illuminates a cause and effect scenario. *Because* Christ came, we get the privilege of having a relationship with God.

Just remember, Christ is the reason; our being in right relationship and fellowship with God is the result.

Never forget the reason nor the result. Praise God for the reason and worship Him for the result.

Empty Anger

There was a time in my life when I was just mad. I mean mad with no purpose. I'd wake up and just be mad. Ever had a day like that? I was having a day like that and journaled about it on my phone. The overall tone of the entry was pure anger and rage. I have no idea what happened that day, but boy, was I upset! A year ago, I was seething and furious without a purpose. I was angry just because.

I believe anger when channeled correctly can be a powerful tool. Let's stop to discuss what anger is. Anger as defined by dictionary.com is "a strong feeling of displeasure and belligerence aroused by a wrong." See how anger is caused by something. Anger stems from something; it doesn't just awaken in you for no reason. Even though anger can be seen as an effect or the result of a cause, I yet believe it has positive powers.

On this particular day, I was more than likely sulking or pretending to be the victim. My journal ended with the following statement, "Someone told me they'd be happy when they could meet the real me. My reply, hell, me too." See, I wasn't really angry. I was just pouting and demonstrating a defeatist attitude. I'd given up on myself and had no plans, no drive to do anything about the situation I'd found myself in. I was angry with no purpose, just mad because I could be.

Now I'm not saying to be angry and go out and become a vigilante or anything, but if you just have to be angry, be angry, and *do something*! The Bible tells us to be angry and sin not; it doesn't say don't be angry. God displays anger; Jesus displayed anger, and we are made in His image and likeness. However, if you pay attention, they became angry as a result of people and things not functioning or fulfilling plans and purposes (Adam and Eve and others). Jesus became angry when the fig tree didn't fulfill its purpose. So even here, the definition fits. Their anger was awakened because of a wrong. They became displeased with events and responded with action. The Lord kicked Adam and Eve out of the garden, and Jesus cursed the fig tree. So no, don't sin in your anger, but please take action! Do something about the very thing that has caused you to be angry. I believe the difference between a victor and victim is action. Victims are angry about offenses yet do nothing. Victors, however, take action to ensure they have *victory* over the offense.

Has Satan ever made you angry? Has he meddled in your life? Tinkered with your finances? Disturbed your peace? Put a damper on your joy? Has he bothered you in any way? How upset were you? Were you bothered, angry, or flat-out enraged? Some of us would dare say we were pissed! Well, I have news for you. Not that I am in a constant state of anger, but I am angry with the enemy.

For so long, he'd convinced me that I wasn't worth anything. He whispered that my mistakes and sins were too big to be forgiven. My walk with Christ too unstable for Him to use me. Yeah, to think I let him offend me this way makes me angry. Angry enough to take a course of action. Angry enough to respond with correction. Angry enough to take my thoughts captive. Angry enough to announce me as the victor and not the victim. Angry enough to do something about him and his conniving ploys and tactics. See, my anger has pushed me to read my Bible more, to pay better attention at church, to ask questions, to stay in communication with people to not be isolated. Yeah, he made me angry, but in being angry, I'm becoming better.

Don't be an angry victim; do something about the thing that caused you to be angry. Become the victor and take *victory* over the offense. Please remember, I'm not suggesting anyone take criminal matters in your own hands and retaliate. I'm simply saying, do what is in your hands to do, legally and spiritually.

What's in Your Hand?

David and Goliath is one of my favorite Bible stories. To me, it's incredible to think of a little ruddy shepherd boy slaying a giant with something as simple as stones. I'll go ahead and jump ahead and get to the celebratory portion of this entry. David used what was in his hand to defeat the giant! Trust me, that is cause for a celebration.

Giants come into our lives for many reasons, and though they can be daunting in appearance and oh, so uncomfortable, they are personally prescribed to us. My giant isn't comparable to yours neither yours to mine yet another reason to celebrate. Though the giants in our lives cause discomfort, pain, and anguish, they can and should be defeated. Quite often, we feel the need to hyperbolize our giants, exaggerate them, causing us to feel as though we are immediately defeated. We think, remember it's what you think that makes the difference, the giant too great to defeat and lose hope just like Saul and his troops. David, unlike the rest of the men, didn't immediately lose hope. He began to inquire as to what was in store for the man that defeated the giant. He immediately began to see himself as the victor and wanted to know what was on the other side of victory. Isn't that how we should think about our situations and giants? I like the story of the little boy who walked into a room filled with manure. His brother, surprised when he began to dig through it, stopped and asked him why he was digging through it. The boy replied, with all this poop, there must be a pony in here somewhere! That's a good thought process. The boy looked beyond immediate appearance and hoped for something greater on the other side.

As David continued to inquire about this giant and what he could gain for defeating him, his brothers and others shrugged him off and didn't take him seriously. My goodness, let me stop there for a moment. Sometimes, we get caught up on how people perceive us and allow this to become the driving force behind what we do and how we think of ourselves. When you're a little different and called out for a specific purpose, people won't always understand you. Unfortunately, when people don't understand you and the call on your life, they may taunt or belittle you. Don't get stuck there; it's not their fault! We know the story; David was only seen as a little shepherd boy, dirty and smelly. Who would've thought he'd become a king! I promise, someday someone will say, "Anitra, short, little weird Anitra? Who would've thought she'd become a speaker and author!" My reply will most definitely be, "Oh, God knew, and I did too!" Anyway, back to our good friend David.

Being that David was a shepherd, he hadn't had any formal training nor did he wear armor. As a matter of fact, Saul put it on him, and he complained that he wasn't comfortable. See, this is where I can see God speaking us telling us to be comfortable in who He has called us to be and His purpose for our lives. You don't have to become a tongue-speaking, Holy Ghost dancing saint to defeat your giant. No, be you and take God with you. That's it; that's all. David didn't try to immediately transform himself from a shepherd to a warrior. No, he went into battle just as he was—a shepherd boy. When you go into battle, know who you are in God and the power that works in you. As the story ends, David used a slingshot and a smooth stone to defeat Goliath. The Bible tells us he picked up five, but he only used one. He used what was in his hand.

So, my friend, what's in your hand? What are your five stones? What do you have that positively affects the kingdom? What is your go-to when things are tough? Prayer should be one of these things. Maybe you sing, maybe you dance, maybe you preach, maybe you teach, whatever it is, I dare you to use what's in your hand! I'm not just writing words to make you feel good. I'm writing tonight because I'm using what's in my hand.

Currently, I'm facing some things, and I'm using what's in my hand to defeat the thought that they are insurmountable, too big to deal with. As I write, I write about the God I serve and love. I write about His ability to bring me (and you) out of treacherous situations. Writing is in my hand. It encourages me as it comes out of me. Writing has two effects on me:

1. I begin writing because I feel depressed, anxious, or angry, and by the time I'm finished, I feel better.
2. I write because I need a release. The tears flow; the angst relieved, and then I'm good. I have no doubt writing is what God has given me as a part of my combat plan.

I don't know what's in your hand. Maybe you don't even know. I know prayer is in *everyone's* hand. The point of this text is to simply say, use what's in your hand to defeat life's giants. No, I'm not saying you devise a plan contrary to what God has given you. Remember, David didn't change one piece of who he was. He refused to wear armor and remained true to himself. He was who God purposed for him to be.

The day will come when you are face-to-face with your life's giant. Do you tremble at the thought of it? Do you flee and cower as one with no faith, or do you trust that God has given you what you need to slay your giant? Will you use what is in your hand?

Fish and Bread…It's All I Have

Five loaves of bread and two fish. It was all the boy had, but he gave it to Christ for Him to use as He saw fit. What counts as your five loaves and two fish? What has God given you to give back to Him? In an earlier text, I talked about using what is in your hand. This correlates to this text as well.

The Bible tells of how Jesus spent time teaching a crowd of five thousand. When the time came for them to eat, very few of the people had brought food. The disciples wanted Jesus to send the people into the villages to buy food, but Jesus sent them out to find people who'd brought food. They discovered this small boy with five loaves of bread and two fish.

- Point 1: You have to be willing to be found.

    The boy was right where God needed him to be when He needed him to be there. When God needs you, will He be able to find you, or will you be somewhere off task?

- Point 2: Don't discredit what you have to offer.

    When they found the boy, the disciples asked Christ, "What is this among so many?" In my mind, they were like, *What can we do with this little amount of food?* Though they were skeptical of his offering, the boy wasn't intimidated by what could be seen as little, inferior, or unable to meet a need. He yielded what he had for Christ to use. Will you yield what you have, or will you hold it for fear it is not enough? By the way, don't compare your gift to anyone else's. Your gift is what God gave you, and theirs is what He gave them.

- Point 3: Allow God to bless your gift.

    Once the boy surrendered his offering unto Christ for Him to use as He saw fit, Christ *blessed* it and used it to feed the people. Now your gift may never provide a physical meal for people; *however,* we know we need spiritual food just as we need physical food. Your offering or gift is made to draw others to Christ. Are you willing to surrender it to Him and allow Him to bless it?

- Point 4: Know that your offering is precious to God.

    Let's see, how do I put this? When you take God your offering, it is precious to Him. After the five thousand had eaten, believe it or not, there were *leftovers*! Now Christ could have just walked away and left the leftovers there, but He commanded His disciples to gather it that *nothing* be lost! How amazing. What started as small ended up being more than enough. *Wow!* Look at that! When you give God your gift, He will bless it and make sure that it is more than enough to meet the need for which it was purposed.

In my mind, that little boy must have been jumping for joy at the thought that Christ could and would use him…just as he was…with what he had in his hand (think David and Goliath). I promise this is for me as much as it is for you. You see, I am gifted and talented. Going to jump out there and be as honest as possible. God has gifted me with the ability to write, sing, and even speak, but you see, I hold back on the singing and speaking for fear that my "five loaves and two fish" aren't good enough. I should take a lesson from this little boy and surrender, shouldn't I? Yeah, well, you should, too, and quickly!

ANITRA FREENEY

Out of Hiding

One of my favorite medleys to listen to is Tye Tribbett's song "Out of Hiding/How He Loves/Good Good Father." I love this song! From the very first time I heard it, I knew I loved it. The message present in this song gives me chills and just makes me feel so, so good!

The first two verses affirm me in such a way it puts a smile on my face. To paraphrase, the vocalist begins the song by saying how safe you are in God, how you can come out of hiding. There is no need to attempt to cover what you think are failures and disappointments. Her second verse just adds icing to the cake. She sings of how there is no fear in God and how He is simply awaiting the day we throw caution to the wind and fall madly in love with Him.

In my earnest opinion, I don't think we can ever love God as much as He loves us. I think it is virtually impossible. Some may disagree, and I'm okay with that. God's love extends beyond our faults, failures, issues, doubt, and even the things that cause us to feel shameful and defeated. God's love is all we'll ever need. It's His love that grants grace and mercy, His love that causes favor to overtake issues and situations. His love covers us. His love is *amazing*!

Anyway, back to the song, if those two verses didn't move you, maybe the chorus will, "'Cause I loved you before you knew it was love. I saw it all, still, I chose the cross. You were the one I was thinking of when I rose from the grave. Now rid of the shackles. My victory is yours. I tore the veil for you to come close. There's no reason to stand at a distance anymore. You're already loved!"

When I sit and think about this song and its implications, I find that I'm in awe of God's love. You see, everything we are and ever will be stem from His love for us. If you know anything about salvation, you know it's a gift by which we can stand in grace and mercy. By way of this gift, we have the opportunity to have a right and loving relationship with God. Without salvation, we have and are nothing. It was love that enabled Christ to die on the cross. It's His love that awakens us each day. It's love that keeps and sustains us through the day and throughout our lives. It's His love that allows us to even love ourselves and then others.

So in the song, when they speak of coming out of hiding, I think of Adam and Eve. They hid when they found out they were naked. They felt ashamed because of the choice they'd made to disobey God. Such is the case with us. When we sin and use poor decision-making skills, we want to tuck tail and run from God. Silly us; don't we realize there is *no* hiding from God? He is omniscient and omnipotent. Don't we realize it is God's providential and intentional love that allows Him to see us but not see us? You see, when He sees us, He sees us as the individuals He has called and purposed us to be, not the silly folk who sin daily. We are constantly and thankfully hidden behind the blood of His son.

So why come out of hiding? Think about the game hide-and-seek. You hide to keep the person from finding you and losing the game. Once everyone but you have been found, you are safe to come out of hiding and win the game. Our lives are no game, but when we liken our situations to this game, we can see how safe it is to come out of hiding. Once we accept Christ as our personal Lord and Savior, we are safe. We are safe to come out of hiding, flaws and all. There is no shame in Christ. There is no defeat in Him. There is no reason to hide. His love extends beyond the things that would cause us to hide.

I'd dare say, standing before God and acknowledging just how much you want to hide and live a life of shame makes Him want to move on your behalf just that much more. God deals in humility and honesty. When we stand "naked" before God and accept His love, He is glorified. Previously, I wrote a text about peeling back layers. Layers enable us to hide. Putting on airs and masks allow us to hide and pretend to be someone we are not.

Some of the questions I'm constantly asking myself on my journey are, *Who are you for real? Like when you're all alone in your thoughts, how do you see yourself? Does your vision of yourself match God's vision?* Today, I must be honest and say, the way I see myself doesn't always match the purpose and plan God has for me. I'm guilty of hiding, not hiding my whole self but hiding gifts and talents for fear I won't measure up. I know the truth. The truth is my gifts and talents are my portions assigned by God. I shouldn't be concerned with matching up to someone else. This is a sin for I'm coveting what someone else has. Shameful, right? Nope…not at all. Just a layer that needs to fall off. Remember, there is no shame in God! It's in realizing you're hiding that you can come out and live the life God has called you to live.

So how do you come out of hiding? You present yourself, your whole self before God in your present state. One of my favorite scriptures is Colossians 2:10 which when paraphrased simply means you are lacking nothing in Christ. He is the final authority, and when He says you are fearfully and wonderfully made, that's it. That's the final word. That scripture, Psalm 139:14, doesn't have a caveat. It doesn't go on to say, you're fearfully and wonderfully made only if you are sinless. *No*! You are fearfully and wonderfully made because God, in His infinite wisdom, created you that way. So why hide? Why take the amazing person you are and hide? To hide means to keep or prevent others from seeing. We aren't a surprise that should be hidden. We are carefully planned and intricately woven beings. For every person on this earth, there is a specific purpose and calling. Why take that and hide it?

We are light in a world of darkness. Matthew 5:15–16 says, "Neither do they light a lamp and put it under a basket, but on a lampstand, and it gives light to all who are in the house. Let your light so shine before men, that they may see your good works and glorify your Father in Heaven."

When we hide our lights, for whatever reason, we deny an opportunity for God to be glorified, which is a dangerous thing. I would compare it to quenching the Holy Spirit…again, a dangerous thing to do and a dangerous situation to find yourself in.

So do yourself a favor; come out of hiding and accept the love God has for you. Don't keep putting your unique and necessary light under a basket!

The love of God is something I've struggled with for quite some time. In my opinion, I've messed up too much, hid far too long to be loved by Him. I now know this to be a lie straight from the pit of hell, and I refute it with the Word! I am loved by God. You are loved by God.

Prayer

Dear God, thank you that in you I am complete and lacking no good thing. When the enemy's whispers suggest I am no good, help me to remember I can do all things through you who gives me strength. Let me not lean to my own understanding but to trust in you. Help me to delight myself in you trusting and believing you will give me the desires of my heart.

In the name of Jesus, amen!

Reflections

After reading Chapter 4,

_____
_____
_____
_____
_____
_____
_____
_____
_____
_____
_____
_____
_____

Chapter 5

A Renewed Mindset

"And do not be conformed to this world, but be transformed by the renewing of your mind, that you may prove what *is* that good and acceptable and perfect will of God."
—(Romans 12:2)

Renew...Reestablish...Reset

I have been reading, studying, and listening to various teaching, and it seems like everything goes back to needing to renew *my* mind, so I write this from a personal perspective. I write this to answer questions I have. Writing is therapeutic for me, so here goes...

There are a ton of things we can renew. We can renew our license, lease, insurance, subscription, membership, and even library cards; however, none of these renewals are as important as renewing your mind.

"Don't become so well-adjusted to your culture that you fit into it without even thinking. Instead, fix your attention on God. You'll be changed from the inside out. Readily recognize what he wants from you, and quickly respond to it. Unlike the culture around you, always dragging you down to its level of immaturity, God brings the best out of you, develops well-formed maturity in you." (Romans 12:2 MSG)

In my mind, to renew means to make new again. You know the basics of affixes; the prefix *re* means again, right? This definition works in the context of the sentence. It makes a lot of sense. So we have to make our minds new again. Okay, I can dig that, but once we make them new again, what should our perspective be? What thoughts should replay in our minds? What should we think about? How does this mind renewal result in God bringing the best out of us?

When we renew a subscription or membership, we reestablish it. Well, what happens when we renew our minds? How exactly do we reestablish it, and what does that mean? To renew our minds is to simply reestablish our thinking to the thoughts of Christ. This is how we don't conform to the world. Christ's works and words were always in direct contradiction to the world's way. When we renew our minds, we go back to thinking how God wanted us to. We focus on His Word; we rid ourselves of our stinking thinking. Our thoughts mirror His Word. In other words, we take on the mind of Christ. Instead of facing tasks with an "I can't do this outlook," we look at it and declare, "I can do all things through Christ who gives me strength." We become lovers of men, sharers of the Gospel, peacemakers, and examples of godliness here on earth. We exemplify a life based on the Gospel, not a life based on fly-by-night emotions or ideas. I'd dare say, a renewed mind is one that defeats every whisper of the enemy with God's Word. This renewed mind doesn't do anything without first consulting God. A reestablished mind goes back to its first love, Christ. When you have this mindset, God can do great things, like bringing the best out of you and developing well-formed maturity in you.

I have to stop and acknowledge I quite often suck at renewing my mind. Frankly, I get stuck in my mind, which is a huge red flag that daily I don't renew it. I can be honest and say, sometimes instead of renewing it, I rehearse things—rehearse what it felt like when my heart was broken, rehearse the devastation of Muh's passing, rehearse the anger I've held against people, rehearsed harsh words shared, lies spread, and whispered gossip. This, my friends, is *not* a renewed mind. It is the opposite. I'm guilty of not allowing God to transform me because I'm too stuck on yesterday!

I attended a training this summer that focused on a fixed mindset in comparison to a growth mindset. A fixed mindset is one that refuses to accept any new truths. A fixed mindset is one that has a defeatist attitude; nothing in their life is and won't be right. They are who they are, and that's just what it is. In comparison, a growth mindset is one that meets each challenge prepared to learn something new. It challenges truths; it bends, moves, and flexes in an attempt to understand better. It knows there is more than one way to skin a cat.

Biblically, a mind not renewed has a fixed mindset. It is locked into the past, locked into defeat, hurt, anger; it is a mind that conforms to a world of hurting people. It is a mind that relies on the saying, "When in Rome, do as the Romans." However, a renewed mind exemplifies a growth mindset. It meets every day with anticipation of how the Word is going to work. It leaves yesterday's failures in the past. It presses on believing God for the better. It applies the Word and sits back and waits on God to show it. It doesn't do as the Romans just because it is in Rome. No, it proudly does the opposite of the Romans and dares them to utter a word. This renewed mind goes and disrupts the norm.

While I have to admit I quite often slip into an unrenewed mind, I am grateful that God brought it to my attention. Where I used to see defeat, I can now choose to see God saying, I have better. I can now combat every yucky situation with the Word. That, my friends, is a renewed mind—one that continues to see God at work. It is reestablished with His plan and purpose. It is restored. It has had a factory reset. It has gone back to its original state so that it can function at maximum capacity.

Stepping Out Like Peter

Stepping out has many different meanings, but the one to which I am referring is the one that involves being moved from your comfort zone. I'm not exactly sure how we develop a comfort zone, but I think we can all agree that our comfort zones are just that—comfortable. What if I said being comfy in your comfort zone is a sign of a faithless and sedentary or inactive life?

Faith, complete trust in God, requires us to move toward things we don't even see yet. It mandates that we trust God even in the face of what seems impossible. Faith and a comfort zone aren't compatible. They just don't work together. I don't think it possible to maintain faith in a comfort zone. Exercising faith should make us uncomfortable, don't you think? Think about Peter walking on the water.

Peter was called (notice the word called…let's ponder on that a moment) out of a boat to do what he deemed impossible: walking on churning and tumultuous water. As long as Peter trusted what Jesus said *and* kept his eyes on Christ, he was fine, but the moment he looked at the waves underneath him, he started to sink. *Oh wee!* Let's stop a moment and talk about our waves.

The waves underneath us may be the words people have uttered about us, the thoughts of failure, the whispers of the enemy, or even a defeatist attitude. Our waves may be different, but they all fulfill the same duty: they cause us to fear instead of faith.

I started this text because I have felt a tug at my heart lately. I am an avid lover of music and singing, but there is this *giant* fear that, quite often, stops me from singing solos or publicly. I'm not saying I am the next recording artist, but I am capable and willing to sing as long as I'm not at the forefront, but as of late, I think God wants that to change. That's not the only area though. It seems that in a lot of areas in my life, I feel the need to be a bit more outgoing, vocal, brave. In other words, I feel the need to not only step out of my comfort zone but to also destroy it!

You see, if I remain in my comfort zone or box, I don't have to lean on God for anything. As long as I remain silent and don't tell my story, as long as I only praise God in private through song, as long as I keep my testimony to myself, I'm hiding in my comfort zone and not stretching as faith requires. I'm not "walking on water." So why do I remain in my boat, my comfort zone? One word: fear. Like Peter, my eyes are stuck on the churning waves beneath me. Now I know

I'm not alone in this. I heard a quote one day, and I can't give credit because I don't remember who said it, but the statement was, "Where there is fear, there is no faith." Sigh…what a devastating thought! In my comfort zone, I have failed to allow faith to bloom and transform me. How do I handle this? How do we, comfort zone dwellers, learn to walk on our personal waters? It's simple, faith instead of fear.

I had a conversation with an incredibly wise woman about this very issue, and with gentle eyes and tone, she looked at me and said, "So your reputation is more important than God's? Do you think He would let you step out on faith in Him and fail? His name is on the line, not yours." *Ouch!* Talk about a moment of reckoning. I had esteemed myself higher than God, thinking I'm too good to jump out there in faith! Here is what I believe she was conveying to me. When we operate in faith and obedience, God is obligated to fulfill His promise to keep us and never fail us. If we have faith and believe in His Word, whatever He has called us to will prosper.

I'd like to suggest to you that like Peter, God is calling us out on the water to trust Him. Will you listen to your waves or the assurances of God and continue walking toward Him?

It's the Thought that Counts

It's the thought that counts is one of those sayings that is typically used to cover up something that went awry. Most of the time, it is used to excuse a poorly-judged gift or something of the like. What if I told you that saying has a biblical basis? When I reread David and Goliath, it became apparent that it's the thought that counts.

David and Goliath is one of my favorite Bible stories. To me, it's incredible to think of a little ruddy shepherd boy slaying a giant with something as simple as stones. Such a small thing for what was thought of as such a large thing.

When I read the story of David and Goliath, one thing stuck out. The Bible says, when they saw Goliath, Saul and his troops lost hope. The mere thought and sound of this giant making a speech caused them to lose hope. Here is what I noticed, and God, I hope I'm right. The troops never even devised a plan. They simply watched him make the same speech twice a day for forty days. That is eighty days' worth of being stuck in fear! No attempt to tackle the problem, just sheer fear and worry. Wow!

Now let's relate this to us. At some point in your life, maybe even now, something is taunting you: a thought, an issue, a problem, a what-if, a failed attempt, fear to even attempt. There is or will be something. Are you frozen in fear at the mere thought of it? Has it caused you, like Saul and his troops, to become paralyzed? Are you simply sitting back and marveling at how large it seems? It's absolutely mind-blowing to me that one smooth stone defeated a giant. Such a small remedy for something perceived so large it stunned an entire army. So what was the problem? Why didn't Saul and his troops think of something so simple? They had wrong thinking.

At the sight of the giant, they took on a defeatist attitude and became quitters (if only y'all knew how bad this is beating me up right now. I'm stepping on my toes!). They thought the giant too large to fight. The crazy part is, even Goliath knew. He didn't want the whole army, just one man. Little David, the shepherd boy, came along and, though they disregarded him, slew the giant. The conversation between David and Saul brings another thing to the forefront. David thought little of the giant because he'd had experience defeating things that were larger than him in the past. The text tells us that David relied on the same God that had delivered him and his sheep from bears' claws and lions' teeth. Man is that powerful! He didn't take any extra steps or drastic methods to go in and slay Goliath. He went in just as he'd tended his sheep—with a slingshot and stones. David had the right thinking.

What do you think about the things you're facing? Do you think the same God who has been with me before is the same God who is yet with me? Do you stare at your giant and lose hope? It's the thought that counts. The power of the mind is incredible. When we ruminate or fixate on an issue, it's comparable to meditating on it. Meditation helps to esteem something or to make it larger and bring all focus to it, meaning it is at the forefront of your mind and guides your every decision and or movement. It's like taking a magnifying glass to enhance the size of something. Get my point? This, in my mind, is how we make mountains out of molehills and giants out of gnats.

Take control of your thinking. David did. He thought about the God he served and took that into battle with him. He ruminated on how God had delivered him in the past. He meditated on God, his deliverer and trusted that He wouldn't fail him. Chances are, your giant can be slain easily by what's in your hand.

Chances are you've magnified your problem by focusing on it instead of the problem solver. Have you meditated on how God is a problem solver, or have you been focusing on your problem instead? I promise, this text right here is stepping all on my toes! Quite often, we begin to tremble at the mere thought of a problem. We stop dead in our tracks and repeat to ourselves how bad the problem is, how we just can't figure it out, how we just don't know what we are going to do. We edify our problem, and all it needs is something as simple as a smooth stone. I won't dare try telling you what these stones signify, but I will tell you that in my mind, the five smooth stones are a representation of the tools God gives us to defeat our fears. The stones were simply what David had in his hand, though he only used one! Combined with his knowledge of God, his deliverer, the stone was used to knock down a giant, but to signify the death of the issue, he cut his head off with his own sword, mind you! Whatever your giant, there is a simple remedy. Change your thinking about it! See it as an opportunity to trust the same God you've trusted in the past. Don't stop dead in your tracks at the sight of an issue, just trust God and stand in who He has called you to be, and face your giant. For so long, Goliath tormented Saul and his troops. For forty days, they were terrified. How long have you been terrified?

Declare today that it ends. David is a great example of focusing on God instead of Goliath. Choose today to focus on God instead of your Goliath. Here is what we know: a Goliath can easily be defeated once you get your mind right! It's the thought that counts!

Prayer

Dear God, I thank you for your Word that urges me to be a nonconformist. I thank you that you don't leave me to figure it out but give me direct instructions. You tell me to renew my mind. Father, forgive me for not renewing my mind and becoming conformed to this world. Thank you that daily, I have another chance to get it right with you. Thank you for your love that continues even when I mess up. Thank you, God, for teaching me how to renew my mind. Now Father, I pray that these words won't sit idle in my mind but that I would develop a growth mindset and daily seek to do better than the day before. Help me to leave yesterday in the past, praise you for the present, and have faith for the future. Father, it is my prayer that you will continue to prune me even though it hurts. I pray that my walk with you would get better and that you may bring out the great things lying dormant in me.

In the name of Jesus, I pray. Amen!

Reflections

After reading Chapter 5,

_____
_____
_____
_____
_____
_____
_____
_____
_____
_____
_____
_____
_____
_____

Chapter 6

Moving On

> Brethren, I do not count myself to have apprehended; but one thing I do, forgetting those things which are behind and reaching forward to those things which are ahead.
> —Philippians 3:13 (NKJV)

The Forgotten Apology

I was at work earlier this week and had a mind-blowing thought. As I sat during my planning period and fell into a deep daydream, I began to analyze a current predicament and picked it apart, separating the issue based on my faults and the faults of others. Then I had to stop and bring myself back to reality, and that's when it hit me. What will happen if I forgive myself? I mean, forgive myself. You know, like, bring back to remembrance every little thing I've done to devalue and belittle myself. How would my life, self-esteem, and self-confidence increase if I stopped looking back at what did happen or even what I allowed to happen?

You see, at some point, it became a habit to apologize to everyone often. If it looked like they were about to be upset, I'd apologize. If I thought there was a misunderstanding, I'd apologize. If there was an apology to be rendered, I'd render it, but I've never stopped and apologized to myself, let alone truly forgiven myself. I can be honest and say, I've carried some things around for quite a while.

I've honestly harbored a twinge of hatred toward myself. Seems like I've always been run over, made fun of, ridiculed for being different, and even talked about (gasp). Subconsciously, I took each of these things in and tucked them away in my "this is all my fault" cabinet and allowed them to fester. Now I'm at a point where I owe myself an apology.

You may ask yourself, "What does she need to apologize for?" You see, I need to apologize for being foolish and allowing my past actions and even the actions of others dictate the kind of person I am and am to be. Believe it or not, there was a time in my life when I'd go hang out and hold on to your pants, *dance*. I used to love to dance. As a matter of fact, I danced from prekindergarten up to sixth grade! I used to have some moves, *but* I, after internalizing the words of others, shut down (I have a bad habit of this). I quit being true to the essence of who I am. I started questioning the very things I held true about myself and adopted an "I'm not good enough" mentality.

While it seems that this is a simple battle of thought process, being a believer of Christ, I fully recognize this as what it truly is. Ephesians 6:12 reads, "For we wrestle not against flesh and blood, but against principalities, against powers, against the rulers of the darkness of this age, against spiritual hosts of wickedness in the heavenly places." Knowing full well that my battle isn't against others, let alone myself, there must be some changes made, and it all starts with apologizing to myself.

> Self,
>
> I'm so sorry. I'm sorry I allowed the whispers of the enemy to deter us from pursuing and walking in the greatness that God has placed within us. I'm sorry I've never fully embraced the uniqueness that is us. I'm sorry I've doubted how fearfully and wonderfully made we are. I'm sorry. I'm sorry I've allowed the words of others to stop us. I'm sorry. I'm so sorry I've shut down and forfeited many an opportunity to exemplify that anointed person God has equipped us to be.

I'm sorry. I'm sorry I've been my very own dream killer. I'm sorry. I'm sorry I've allowed past mistakes to dictate future endeavors.

Self, I'm so sorry. Would you please find it within you to forgive me so we can move forward? It's far past time I've delivered this apology. It's far past time I, through the power of the Holy Spirit, break this stronghold and free myself from this imaginary jail cell. Time has been far spent stuck in this mental cage. Self, again, I apologize. I'm so sorry. Now let's go; be great and show God just how much we appreciate His love, His mercy, His grace, His peace, and His deliverance. Let's stop reliving things of the past and make room for new memories of great triumphs, accomplishments, and victories!

Sidenote: I truly had this conversation with myself. I truly feel like, at times, we must stop and simply apologize to ourselves. Of course, as I typed this, the tears fell. I've been writing on and off for about five years now, and I have to say, this is my most heartfelt entry. I hope it blesses you as much as it blessed me.

I Hereby Resign

To Whom It May Concern:

This letter is to inform you of a major shift in my life. I, Anitra Lachelle Freeney, being of sound mind do declare that I'm resigning my position effective immediately. Unfortunately, there is no time to give a two weeks' notice, and for this, I do *not* apologize. You see, I must vacate this position immediately. Far too long have I resigned myself to a life that is subpar and in direct opposition to the life God has called, equipped, and predestined me for. Afraid of stepping out of my comfort zone and doing things a different way, I stayed in my little box where I felt I had everything under control, and things were going positively and methodically.

This new mindset doesn't come haphazardly or without merit. You see, my eyes have been opened. Friday, I took part in a social-emotional learning training session in which I broke down and cried...in front of my principal and numerous staff members (trust me; I had a good reason). What I learned in that training is, stepping out of my comfort zone is as simple as taking *one* step followed by another, and another, and another. It doesn't even require any formal training to break free. In the words of my pastor, ain't that something?

To the person reading this letter, it is imperative that I step down and prayerfully leave this position vacant. Should I choose to remain in this position, my life will continue to be stagnant and lack what I feel are drive and initiative. So again, I must resign effective immediately. I have received a promotion, and I simply have to broaden my horizon and do what God has called me to do. No longer can I remain silent about His goodness, grace, mercy, and most importantly, His love. You see, it was that love that even enables me to have the strength to resign from this position and pursue greater endeavors and experiences.

Fear, doubt, insecurity, inferiority, self-consciousness, food addiction, bipolar, anxiety, whichever one of you should read this letter, just know I'm done. I simply cannot continue on the path that I am currently on. It has not been a pleasurable experience, and I make the conscious decision to end our relationship right now. Somehow, someway, you bamboozled me into believing this position was the best I could do. Somehow you tricked me; you fooled me into thinking I was stuck, unable to do better, unable to live a better life, forced to wear titles and have negative things attached to my name. You could not have been anymore inaccurate! Everything you limited, God wants to expand. Everything you kept secret, God wants to expose, and I'm all for that!

For so long, you've crippled me, kept me from living my best life, and being great. I'm tired of being tired. I simply cannot continue in this manner. There is so much more for me out there, and I must be purposeful about acquiring the great things God has prepared for me. So you see, I've outgrown this position. My knowledge has been broadened, my skills enhanced, and I simply must resign. It is time for us to part ways. No longer can I stay in this dead-end situation.

I'm certain this news comes as a surprise, but it's time. At thirty-eight, I no longer have time for neither foolishness nor fruitless journeys.

It is with a humble heart, zeal, and a spirit of excellence that I render my resignation.

Warmest regards,
Anitra L. Freeney

A Word from the Author

It is my sincere hope and prayer that this book has strengthened your faith and belief in God. I'm filled with great anticipation as I think of the endless possibilities for your life.

Perhaps you realize you need to accept Christ as your personal Lord and Savior. Please turn to the next page and simply recite the prayer of salvation. Please know there is no magic in the words. The power comes in your belief that God is who He says He is!

If this book has sparked a desire in you to rededicate your life to Christ, there is a prayer just below the prayer of salvation.

May everything you touch prosper! In the words of my pastor, Rev. Kennon L. Tenison, "Go be great!"

Tons of love and inspiration your way,
Anitra L. Freeney

Prayer of Salvation

Dear God, I acknowledge that I've lived my life apart from you as a sinner. I come to you today with full belief in the death, burial, and resurrection of your Son, Jesus Christ. I believe He did these things as a payment for my sins. I choose this day to turn away from my life of sin and turn to you for your love and sanctification. I ask that you would come into my life and heart. Help me to trust you fully as my Lord and Savior.

In the name of Jesus, I pray.
Amen!

Prayer for Rededication

Dear God, I come to you asking that you reignite my passion for you. Help me to once again trust you fully and without hesitation. I thank you for moving into my heart and allowing me to trust you as my Lord and Savior. Please forgive me for leaning to my ways and understanding. Help me to hold fast to your uncompromising Word and promises.

In the name of Jesus, I pray.
Amen!

About the Author

Ms. Anitra L. Freeney is a born-again baptized believer in Jesus Christ. She attended both undergraduate and graduate school at Dallas Baptist University where she received her BA in elementary education and MEd in reading education with a specialization in English as a second language and has currently been accepted into Northcentral University's doctorate program. She currently serves as a fourth-grade teacher.

Although she has battled with the diagnosis of bipolar disorder, she has learned to combat spells of depression with the Word of God and esteems herself in it daily.

As a single woman, Anitra lives a quiet life, spending her spare time reading, blogging, and enjoying music.

CPSIA information can be obtained
at www.ICGtesting.com
Printed in the USA
LVHW090205110621
689980LV00005B/48